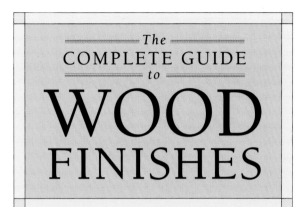

The

COMPLETE GUIDE

to

WOOD
FINISHES

The
COMPLETE GUIDE
to
WOOD
FINISHES

DERRICK CRUMP
CONSULTANT *Ronnie Rustin*

 SIMON & SCHUSTER
AUSTRALIA

The complete guide to wood finishes

First published in Australia in 1993 by
Simon & Schuster, Australia
20 Barcoo Street, East Roseville, NSW 2069

Reprinted 1995

Viacom International
Sydney, New York, London, Toronto, Tokyo, Singapore

National Library of Australia
Cataloguing in Publication data
Crump, Derrick.
The complete guide to wood finishes

Includes Index
ISBN 0 7318 0411 2
1. Furniture finishing. I. Title.
684.1043

This book was designed and produced by
Quarto Publishing plc
The Old Brewery
6 Blundell Street
London N7 9BH

SENIOR EDITOR Kate Kirby
EDITOR Nick Gibbs
COPY EDITOR Peter Leek
SENIOR ART EDITOR Penny Cobb
DESIGNER Terry Jeavons
PICTURE RESEARCHER Anne Marie Ehrlich
PHOTOGRAPHER Paul Forrester
ILLUSTRATOR Rob Shone
ART DIRECTOR Moira Clinch
PUBLISHING DIRECTOR Janet Slingsby

Typeset in Great Britain by Bookworm Typesetting, Manchester
Printed in Singapore by Star Standard Industries Private Ltd
Manufactured in Hong Kong by Regent Publishing Services Ltd

Special thanks to Andy Hills, Tony Miller and Katie Preston.

Publisher's note

Working with wood finishes demands care, as some of the chemicals you will be using are poisonous and/or corrosive. This means you must take precautions when handling them: always follow the manufacturer's instructions; always store chemicals securely in clearly marked non-food containers and keep them well out of reach of children.

As far as the composition of the finishes mentioned in this book, the techniques used to apply them, and the effects they produce are concerned, all statements, information and advice given here are believed to be true and accurate. However, neither the author, copyright holder nor the publisher can accept any legal liability for errors or omissions.

Acknowledgements and picture credits

QUARTO would like to thank the following for their help with this publication and for permission to reproduce copyright material.

KEY l = left, r = right, a = above, b = below.

P. 61	Lawrence Kemp/*Forgotten Finishes*/photo Loraine Freeman
P. 69	Howard Raybould
P. 79	Non-drip varnish with Teflon/Natural Wood Finishes from Dulux
P. 89	Elrose Products Ltd/Infopress
P. 99	Crown Paints
P. 101 l	Elrose Products Ltd/Infopress
r	Lawrence Kemp/*Forgotten Finishes*/photo Loraine Freeman
P. 110 l	Crown Paints
r	Elrose Products Ltd/Infopress
P. 111 b	Elrose Products Ltd/Infopress
P. 117 a	A. Holmes/Crafts Council
b	Crown Paints
P. 145	Crown Paints

Every effort has been made to trace and acknowledge all copyright holders. Quarto would like to apologise if any omissions have been made.

QUARTO would like to thank the following organizations who kindly lent equipment for photography.

The Art Veneers Co. Ltd.: *veneers.*

Axminster Power Tools Centre: *power sanders and accessories, soldering irons, ear protectors, stopping knives.*

Bolloms: *Spray equipment.*

F.A. Heffer & Co. Ltd.: *badger brush, mottler brush.*

John Mylands: *safety equipment, abrasives, brushes, sanding belt, sponge.*

Stanley Tools: *hand scrapers, scalpels, clamps, chisels, drill.*

CONTENTS

Decorative finishes . . 84-123

Spray finishes 124-149

Guide to woods 150-163
Troubleshooting 164-167
Health and safety . . . 168-169

FOREWORD

Wood looks dull and unattractive until it has been finished with materials that will preserve, protect and bring out the inherent beauty of the grain. For thousands of years the only treatment was to apply beeswax, oils, or to colour the woods with a mixture of pigments and binders to hold the pigment on the surface. Now there is an extremely large range of wood finishing products available, many for specific uses, such as on floors, others which can be used for a variety of purposes. There are also finishes specifically made for furniture and cabinet work where the highest of finish is required.

There has always been a mystique about wood finishing but with the modern materials available the amateur can obtain results that in most cases are far superior to the finishes seen on mass produced furniture.

Remember that however well made an article may be, it is by the final finish that it is judged. The surface must be clean, smooth and free from all blemishes as unless the surface is being painted any imperfections will be made more apparent when a finish is applied. The main processes in finishing are filling, stopping, staining and applying the finish. Bleaching may also be necessary to remove stains in the wood or to lighten it. If you are renovating a piece and the original finish is in a very bad condition then the only satisfactory treatment is to strip it completely, preferably with a solvent paint and varnish remover, and to start again as if it were new wood.

Wood finishes which leave a surface film are of three main types. They can dry either by 1) evaporation of the solvents, as with French polish or cellulose lacquers; 2) oxidization and polymerization by absorbing oxygen from the air, as with linseed and other drying oils; or 3) by cross-polymerization, that is the linking together of the molecules after the addition of the catalyzt, as occurs with acid-catalised cold-cure lacquers and two-part polyurethanes. The latter type of product will give the most durable surface and it will also be resistant to heat, solvents and abrasions. When you are considering what type of finish to apply bear in mind to what use the piece you are finishing will be put. For instance, it is not worth using an expensive two-part lacquer on wall cladding that will not be subjected to the same wear and tear as will a floor or a table top. The golden rule is always to read the manufacturer's instructions, and if using a finish of which you have had no previous experience to experiment on a spare piece of wood.

It is often possible to buy old furniture from antique shops and junk shops, as well as from auctions, and as long as the basic construction is sound, the finish can be restored to its original or better condition, usually without having to strip back to the bare wood. I once purchased a chair for £8.50 which turned out to be a genuine George III chair and was later valued at over £300. It only required a new upholstered seat and for the finish to be cleaned. On another occasion I purchased for £5 a large Adam-style fireplace surround, which was in a very sorry state. After stripping it I discovered that it had been hand carved and was probably well over 100 years old. Sealed, waxed and restored to its original condition, the fireplace surround is now an object of great beauty, and probably very valuable too.

I hope that you too will find similar bargains, and I am sure that whether you are working on new furniture or restoring old furniture you will have a great sense of satisfaction with the finished results.

Ronnie Rustin

Ronnie Rustin

1

Tools and equipment

Few specialized tools are needed for finishing.

A woodworker with a basic toolkit will

only require a selection of brushes and

cloths. Novices need a work surface

and some scrapers, but little more

Basic tools and equipment

Although one attraction of finishing is the limited selection of tools required, experienced finishers will have built up a sizable toolkit. Novice finishers will not necessarily need a wide range of tools, but certain items, which may not at first seem obvious, are essential aids to successful finishing.

The scalpel is perhaps one of the most underrated of tools. Often, only the point is used for cutting, but the sharp edge can also be useful for gently scraping unwanted finishes or marks from a surface. Masking tape is useful when you need to protect a particular area while finishing another. Cover the sensitive area with tape and cut very gently around the shape. A metal rule will help for straight edges. When cutting through masking tape it is

Natural sponge
▶ A sponge is useful for applying finishes, especially decorative ones.

Hand drill
◀ A drill is useful when hammering in moulding and panel pins that may split the timber.

F-cramp
▲ Do not be tempted to buy a large and unwieldly cramp. A 100mm (4in) cramp is fine.

Soldering iron
▶ For melting shellac stoppers, the soldering iron does not have to be an expensive model. Remember to unplug it after use, and note that even cheap soldering irons get very hot.

better to make multiple cuts, rather than try to cut through with one stroke of the scalpel.

Masking tape can also be used for holding small chips in place while they are being glued. Carry a small F-cramp for those circumstances when tape will not provide enough force.

Other useful tools that are worth buying are a natural sponge, a small drill and a small soldering iron. Natural sponges are better for applying finishes, especially decorative effects, than artificial ones. The drill is useful when hammering in moulding and panel pins that may split the timber. A soldering iron is useful for warming shellac stopper before pushing the stopper into a dent or crack.

Stopping knife
▶ *Tailor-made for applying stopper. Do not let the stopper dry on the knife.*

Chisel
▼ *Chisels are handy for cleaning off glue when working on old pieces.*

Scalpel
▶ *A scalpel is vital for cutting and can also be used for scraping unwanted finish.*

Masking tape
▲ *Masking tape is excellent if you need to protect a particular area while finishing another.*

CLOTHS, MOPS AND WADDING

● White rag, which is sold by weight, is a pure cotton rag that has no starch. It is used for making the skin of a polishing rubber.

● Stockinet is used for polishing, when applying burnishing cream, wax or oil. It is sold by the roll.

● Hessian is a loose-woven sacking, used for applying and taking off grain fillers.

● Skein wadding, available from haberdasheries, is generally used as the core of the polishing rubber. Buy it in a bundle, by length, and store on a roll. Some finishers like to remove the skin before using wadding in a polishing rubber. At a pinch, instead of wadding, cotton wool can be used but it does tend to go soggy.

● Colouring mops are like round-tipped brushes. They are more convenient than cloth for working finishes and stains into mouldings.

● A lamb's wool mop is a round mop used, on a disc, for burnishing.

● An edge mop can be used for burnishing, usually powered by an angle grinder.

Brushes for finishing

SEE ALSO

50–52
BLEACHING WOOD

58–65
FRENCH POLISHING

84–123
DECORATIVE FINISHES

Brushes are an important part of any finisher's equipment, and most suppliers offer a variety of designs for specialist applications. They are made of different bristles and hairs, both synthetic and natural, and there are many names given to these brushes. Generally the higher the price, the better the quality of bristle and brush. In the long run, it is worth purchasing quality brushes. The finest hair commands the highest price, with badger, horse, sable, camel and hog providing the raw materials.

Natural-hair brushes give a fine finish and have a spring in them, which allows the material being coated to cling to the hair. Brush manufacturers use a mixture of bristles to suit requirements. Sable pencil brushes and mops are the most expensive, but bring the best results.

Swan or quill
◀ These are small brushes for touching up.

Mop
▶ These are used for applying stains, colour or polish. Th[ey] are available in siz[es] to 20 and are made from hog or sable.

Mottler
▶ These are used to mottle glazes and scumbles when marbling or graining. They are made from hog hair.

Pencil brush
▼ These are used for touching up and for graining and grain simulation. They are sold in sizes 2 to 10 and are made from camel, sable or synthetic hair.

Wire brush
▼ Useful for opening up the grain when applying a limed finish and for stripping mouldings and carvings.

Badger or softener
▲ These are for "softening in" grain or marble effects. They are made from badger hair.

14

Stencil brush
▼ These are specifically designed for stencilling. They are shaped like shaving brushes and are used with a dabbing action.

Flitch
▼ These are for work on mouldings and edges. They are made from hog hair.

Dulling brush
▼ These, made from short hog hair, are used for dulling down finishes.

Grass brush
▲ These are made from vegetable fibres. They are ideal for bleaching, since ordinary decorating brushes are not resistant to acid and so tend to shed their bristles when used with bleach.

CARE OF BRUSHES

Keep mops and pencil brushes in a polyethylene bag.

Suspend brushes in solvent to soak them clean.

Think of brushes as tools. Look after them properly, and they will last for years and pay for themselves.

Flat *or* paintbrush
◄ These can be used to apply stains, varnish, undercoats and glazes. They are made from hog or horse hair.

Stippling brush
▼ Made from coarse hog-hair bristles and used to produce a decorative stippled effect on timber and other substrates.

Flogger
► These are for use in the graining process and are made from hog hair.

Scrapers

SEE ALSO

18–19
POWERED SANDERS

20–21
ABRASIVES

30–32
REPAIRING VENEERS

Scrapers are used for taking off the finest of shavings, to produce the smoothness of surface not always possible with a plane – or even, some would say, with abrasive. Skilled woodworkers use them as an alternative to a progression of sandpapers or abrasive grades that tend to clog the surface with dust (see pages 20–21). Scrapers are particularly useful for smoothing areas of wild interlocking grain, which a plane might tear; and on veneer, which is vulnerable because of its thinness. They are easier to control than a plane, and can be shaped to work mouldings or corners.

Although there are a variety of scrapers, they are in essence little more than a thin sheet of steel and they cut with a burr – rather than the edge, as a plane blade does. Creating that burr is achieved with a file and burnisher, but care is needed to maintain a scraper in good working order, as it will only cut well if the edge is kept straight and square.

Using a scraper

To use a scraper, hold it in both hands, with your thumbs at the back, and push it across the surface. Alternatively, some people prefer to use a pulling action, with their fingers behind the scraper creating the pressure.

The angle at which the scraper is

Cabinet scraper
▶ The cabinet scraper is the most common version. In its simplest form it is a rectangle of steel, usually about 10 × 5cm (4 × 2in).

Moulding or gooseneck scraper
▶ A development of the cabinet scraper is the moulding or gooseneck scraper, found in a variety of shapes, combining profiles and radii.

Paint scraper
▶ Other types of scraper with a handle are available and are popular in the decorating trades – including, of course, paint scrapers.

held is determined by the angle of the burr. Experiment until thin shavings are produced. By pushing with your thumbs or fingers the scraper can be bent to aid the cut, with a tighter curve producing a narrower cutting area. However, take care not to remove too much material, as it is easy to produce furrows in the surface.

HINTS AND TIPS

- A drop of oil or spit on the burnisher helps during sharpening and gives extra bite.

- Try different angles for sharpening and using the scraper.

- Broken glass makes an effective scraper, but the edge is short-lived and care is needed when breaking it.

Sharpening a scraper
▲ **1** *File the edge of the scraper flat, then run a burnisher along its face to remove any burrs. The edge is now ready to be sharpened.*

Adjustable scrapers
◀▶ *An adjustable scraper has a handle that holds the blade and allows the steel to be worn down to the last.*

▲ **2** *Hold the scraper securely, either in a vice or against the worktop, and rub the burnisher along the edge. As the burr is produced, roll the burnisher over to give the burr a hook of about 5 degrees.*

Using the scraper
▲ *Hold the scraper with your fingers to the back and thumbs to the front. Angle it away from your body, using your thumbs to curve the blade of the scraper, as you push to cut.*

Powered sanders

SEE ALSO

20-22
ABRASIVES

168-169
HEALTH AND SAFETY

Sanders provide the potential for fast stock removal and a fine finish. They come in a variety of shapes and sizes, and there is a range of hand-held and static machines. The former are powered by electricity, battery or compressed air. Of the static machines, belt or pad sanders are the most common. The belts are available in a range of lengths and widths. Lathes can often be fitted with abrasive discs, but by the time a piece has reached the finishing stage it should only need smoothing with a sander.

Portable belt sanders are powerful tools that can easily destroy veneer. They leave obvious marks when used across the grain. Orbital sanders can sand with and across the grain simultaneously, though when sanding with them you should be careful to follow the grain.

An important feature of any sander is some form of suction device to remove the dust into a bag. Wearing a mask when using a sander is recommended in any circumstance, especially when no extraction facility is present.

Disc sanders

▼ *In their crudest form (on angle grinders, for example), sanding discs scratch too deeply for finishing purposes and leave obvious rings. But they are very useful for smoothing curved surfaces on carvings and sculpture – with a rubber backing, they can follow the shape of the piece as no other powered sander can.*

There are also various drumlike sanding accessories that can be attached to a drill. These are particularly popular amongst turners for working on revolving pieces at the lathe.

Sanding accessories to accompany drills

◀ *Accessories such as these are useful for sanding turnings and mouldings.*

Belt sanders

▼ *From a finishing point of view, the only advantage of a belt sander is its ability to remove material quickly from large workpieces. If you use one for abrasive stripping, you will find that it removes paint fast and effectively.*

Never start a belt sander when it is in contact with a workpiece, and always lift it from the workpiece before stopping. Be prepared for a sudden jerk when applying the sander to the surface. The belts, which are supplied in all grades, revolve very fast between two rollers.

Orbital sanders

◀ *Although there are smaller palm and cordless versions, the most common orbital sanders are designed to take a third of an abrasive sheet. The motion drives the sanding plate in an elliptical or random orbit – but, though their light action makes them suitable for finishing work, they tend to leave fine curly scratches. The more sophisticated versions incorporate dust-extraction systems that suck the dust away from the surface and so reduce scratching.*

BOSCH
PBS 75

Abrasives

SEE ALSO

26-27
BRUISES, DENTS
AND SCRATCHES

18-19
POWERED SANDERS

30-31
REPAIRING VENEERS

Types of paper
1 *For rubbing curves and shaped areas, use a flexible abrasive.*
2 *Flour paper used for preparing raw timber and cutting down between coats.*
3 *Self-lubricating silicon-carbide paper can be used for denibbing (rubbing down between coats).*
4 *Glasspaper for sanding raw timber.*
5 *Fine garnet paper is used for working on timber, and between coats of finish.*

It is no longer accurate to describe abrasives as sandpaper, or even glasspaper, as nowadays all sorts of materials are used for abrading wood. Moreover, the range now goes further than paper-backed varieties, with cloth, card and Velcro backings available to suit different types of work. It is therefore worth investigating the various options, as the cheapest and most commonly supplied abrasives found in local hardware stores (usually brown and made from broken bottles) have now been superseded and they produce an inferior finish. They are also more difficult to use, as the abrasive easily becomes detached.

Abrasives are graded by grit size on the back of each sheet – the lower the number, the coarser the grade. You will rarely need abrasive coarser than 80 grit, while at the other end of the scale 240 grit is very fine and is sufficient for preparing surfaces for finishing. You may want to use a finer grade between coats, but note that when machine-sanding the speed of the abrasive over the surface makes each grade more powerful than when sanding by hand.

Woodworkers and finishers often talk about "working through the grades", referring to the technique of using a series of grit grades, progressing from coarse to fine, when preparing a piece. Three steps are normally enough – starting with 100 grit, then changing to 180 grit and finishing with 240 grit. These descriptions of grit grades are not always standard, so look out for alternative methods of grading when selecting abrasives.

Garnet

Garnet remains the most common general-purpose abrasive. By nature it is self-sharpening, with new cutting edges appearing as it breaks down. Although it retains an even cut, it is sometimes worth rubbing garnet paper on a scrap piece of oak or metal before using it on a surface for finishing, as the grit is sharp and can carve out deep scratches. Garnet paper is best used by hand, like glasspaper, as the bond is not strong enough to survive machine sanding. It can be employed for work on either raw or polished timber.

Pumice powder
◄ *Use pumice powder for dulling and as a fine abrasive between applications of French polish. Rub the powder in with a dulling brush or a clean cloth.*

Grades of wire wool
1 Use No. 0 wire wool for dulling with wax.
2 No. 00 wire wool produces a satin finish.
3 No. 000 wire wool is used to obtain a very fine matt effect.
4 No. 0000 wire wool is so fine that, in some circumstances, it glosses the surface.

Cork block
▲ *Use a cork block for sanding flat surfaces by hand. Fold the abrasive around the block and work with the grain. This ensures even preparation and reduces the chance of producing furrows.*

6 Coarse garnet paper is used for preparation.
7 Coarse aluminium-oxide (alox) paper is used for preparation. Fine alox can be used between coats of finish.

Aluminium oxide

Aluminium oxide is the manmade alternative to garnet as a general-purpose abrasive. It is supplied on a variety of backings and can be used for machine sanding as readily as by hand.

Use aluminium oxide with a medium paper backing for hard sanding and with orbital sanders. Its open coat of abrasive allows rapid stock removal with little clogging. Surface scratches when sanding are generally caused by dust particles collecting amongst the grit, so an abrasive that reduces clogging is best for a fine finish.

Cloth-backed aluminium oxide has a longer life and is more flexible than many paper-backed grades. Use the cloth-backed versions when sanding with a disc sander or angle grinder. They should also be used when sanding with abrasive flails, soft drums or pneumatic drums, all of which are excellent for contour sanding.

Silicon carbide

Never is it more important to reduce scratching than when rubbing back between coats of finish. The traditional method is to use soap and water or white spirit. As a modern alternative manufacturers have developed a silicon-carbide paper with a powder substance filling the gaps between the abrasive grains, thus reducing the likelihood of clogging and scratching. It works well for hand and machine sanding.

Wire wool

An alternative to abrasive papers, wire wool has the advantage of being non-clogging. It is available in a range of grades, each suited to a different purpose.

Sanding by hand
▲ 1 *Wipe the surface with a damp cloth to raise the grain.*

▲ 2 *Cut the abrasive sheet into quarters and wrap around a cork block, folding edges sharply.*

▲ 3 *Do not press the block too hard, but follow the grain with even pressure.*

The finishing shop

**STORING TOOLS
AND MATERIALS**

● Fit out the workshop with ample storage space for holding tools, materials, brushes, rags, wadding and abrasives. Flammable finishes and materials must be kept in a lockable cupboard on their own, out of the way.

● Collect airtight containers for storing polishing rubbers and fads for future use. Do not use old food containers (in case the contents are mistaken for food), or milk bottles. Containers should be labelled carefully and dated. Always have a sealable container at hand for waste materials, which must be disposed of safely (see pages 168-169).

The layout, lighting and heating of the workshop play a vital role in achieving a quality finish. Your workshop must be dry and warm, and have plenty of natural light. There are also a number of jigs, fittings, and ideas for benches and storage that make finishing that much easier.

In all probability, your finishing workshop is also used for operations such as sawing and sanding. In which case, you will have to ensure that dust is kept under control. A good extractor or industrial vacuum cleaner helps, but make sure the workshop is free from draughts and that nooks and crannies, which serve as dust traps, are kept to a minimum.

Heating and ventilation

Manufacturers of most finishing materials advise that the minimum temperature at which their products will dry is about 16 °C (60°F). If drying does not take place at the proper rate, defects such as chilling and blushing appear in the surface.

Make sure materials are stored in the workshop for at least an hour before work commences. If it is very cold and you are not able to heat the workshop, use a powerful electric light or a hair dryer to bring the surface temperature nearer to the optimum (the timber will hold the heat for a surprisingly long time).

Finishing materials are designed to flow and are sensitive to heat. If they do not flow, brush marks are likely to create an uneven coat. Make sure there are no cold draughts, but keep the workshop ventilated to cut down condensation.

Lighting

When finishing, you will be continually judging colour and degree of gloss. To be able to do this successfully, it is essential to have a good light source. The best source is, of course, natural light, which defines subtle differences of colour and shade most clearly. This is particularly important when colour matching.

If possible, arrange the workshop with northern light, which is constant and natural. Direct sunlight is not advisable, as judging colour can be tricky in fierce sunlight. Otherwise, the best alternative to the real thing is to fit fluorescent tubes or light bulbs that give a "natural light".

Drying racks

An important feature of any finishing shop is a drying rack. This can either be fixed or portable, but make sure there is plenty of room for air to circulate between the pieces while they are drying. Dowelling jointed into uprights works well for racking, with at least 10cm (4in) between each level. The configuration depends on the type of work you expect to be finishing. For example, chairs need a different set-up to panels – but the principle always remains the same.

The workbench

The workbench can simply be a board on trestles. This helps bring small items and panels up to a convenient height, but can be dismantled when there are large or freestanding pieces in the workshop. Cut up some thin strips of timber on which flat panels can rest while being finished.

23

2

Preparation

No finish is better than its preparation. A smooth and clean surface is essential, as any blemish will be exaggerated by the finish. Use fingers and eyes to check for faults assiduously – but you will soon be able to judge instinctively whether a surface has been adequately prepared

Bruises, dents and scratches

SEE ALSO

18–19
POWERED
SANDERS

30–31
REPAIRING
VENEERS

40–43
HOW TO USE
STOPPERS

80–83
RESTORING OLD
FINISHES

Indentations in the surface are caused either by the compression of fibres (in the case of bruises and dents) or by the fibres being broken by scratches. These faults must be removed before sanding. If the bruises or scratches are deep, it is best to raise them rather than try to sand them out. Heavy sanding is likely to result in an uneven surface, and on a veneered piece it may even break through the veneer.

The principle of raising bruises is to swell the fibres of the timber by sweating with heat and steam. The expansion of the fibres levels the surface. This may not work fully when the fibres are badly broken, especially with deep scratches across the grain, but sweating will at least reduce the amount of filling or sanding needed to produce a surface fit for finishing.

Practice

Place a dampened cloth over the fault and push down gently with a hot iron. This produces steam. If the bruise does not come out at the first attempt, repeat the procedure until it does, rewetting the cloth each time. Take care when working on edges and mouldings: these are easier to damage or burn than flat surfaces, and are often the most badly affected by faults.

Ironing out a bruise
▲ 1 *The picture frame before ironing out the bruises. The mouldings and corners are most likely to be affected by bruising, because they are prominent and their rounded shape makes them vulnerable. You cannot expect scratches to be repaired by steaming, but most bruises respond to this treatment. Make sure that any old finish is thoroughly cleaned off the piece.*

▲ 2 *Dampen the surface around the bruise with a cloth soaked in water. Always check that the water and cloth are clean – it is easy to discolour the wood. Use a clean white cloth, and certainly not one that has been used for staining. Press the cloth against the bruise so that the water soaks into the fibres of the wood, and does not simply run off. Try not to wet too much of the piece. This could lift veneer and weaken joints.*

The bruise removed
◀ *Having steamed out the bruise, leave the surface to dry, and sand with fine abrasive paper.*

◀ **3** *Lay a damp piece of white cloth over the bruise. Experiment by folding the cloth once to start. You may find that it dries out too quickly. In this case, fold the cloth again or adjust the heat control on the iron. Do not use cloth that is too thin, otherwise there is a risk of burning or bruising the piece further.*

◀ **4** *Press the iron on the damp cloth. Make sure the iron is very hot – the steam should not be allowed to disperse before it has entered the wood. Press down with the iron until the steam ceases. Remove the iron and cloth to inspect the bruise. If the bruise is still there, repeat the operation, soaking the cloth with water each time. Leave the surface to dry before further finishing.*

HINTS AND TIPS

• Excess water can be removed by using the hot iron, but keep plenty of dry cloths available.

• Avoid direct contact between the iron and the workpiece, as there is always a risk of burning or further bruising.

MEMO

Safety precautions
You will be using a very hot iron – so arrange your working area carefully, ensuring it is not cluttered and that the iron can be placed out of harm's way when on.

Tools and materials
Cast-iron iron or electric iron

White or colour-fast cloths

Water

Appropriate surfaces
Softwoods react faster than hardwoods to steaming. However, the differences in grain density are more prominent in softer timbers, so check that bruises have been raised thoroughly.

Steaming deep bruises works better on solid wood than on a veneered surface. With veneer, the glue film can act as a barrier to the steam, and the fibres of the substrate may not expand as effectively as with solid timber.

Common problem
Where the fibres have been broken, filling and sanding will be necessary.

Drying time
Bruises can be raised within seconds – but leave the surface to dry before further work.

Dealing with blisters

Blisters in veneer are caused by the veneer lifting, either because air has been trapped beneath it or because the glue spread is faulty. To correct this fault the blister must be burst, which expels the air, then the veneer can be stuck down again with glue.

A similar fault, often found in old furniture, is called tenting. It tends to occur along joins between veneers or on the edges of panels when water or moisture has worked its way under the veneer. Tenting is dealt with in much the same way as a blister, but make sure the groundwork is dry before attempting to glue the veneer down.

Practice

Use a hypodermic syringe to inject glue into the blister. Do not use too much glue, as it is difficult to expel and may be forced beneath the existing bond. You may find it helpful to drill a tiny hole in the blister as a pilot for the syringe.

Another way to deal with a blister is to cut through the veneer, using a veneer knife, scalpel or craft knife. Work glue under the blister, then flatten it with a hot iron. To protect the face of the veneer, put paper between the iron and the workpiece. Take care not to loosen other areas of the veneer with the heat and steam.

Once the repaired blister has dried, sand lightly or use a scraper to remove any glue marks (see pages 16-17). If you cut open the blister with a knife, a slight overlap may need to be sanded flat. Syringe holes sometimes have to be filled (see pages 40-43).

HINTS AND TIPS

● Cut along the grain.

● Use a sharp knife.

● To avoid pulling up the grain, protect veneer with waxed paper or polyethylene when cramping.

● If cramps are used, bridge unsupported areas such as drawer cavities.

Repairing blisters in veneer

▲ **1** *Blisters occur when a veneer has not been pressed down correctly, or because an air bubble has developed. Run your hand over the piece to check for blisters and tap the surface with a finger nail, listening for* *a hollow sound. Blisters cannot be sanded away – the abrasive would break through the thin skin – the veneer must be glued back in place.*

▲ **2** *Cut open the blister with a sharp scalpel or veneer knife to let out the air and allow access for new glue. Cut in the direction of the grain, following the pattern where possible. Try to cut through the veneer* *in one stroke, and avoid cutting into the groundwork.*

▲ **3** *Lift one side of the open blister with the point of the scalpel or veneer knife, and let in the glue using a syringe. Use as little glue as possible to avoid marking the timber and overfilling the blister. Antique veneer was normally glued down* *with Scotch glue, but white PVA is easy to use and readily available.*

▲ **5** *Wipe off any excess glue from the surface of the piece with a damp rag. Glue that has dried on the surface often shows up, even after careful sanding, so it is* *worth cleaning it off while it is still wet.*

▲ **6** *Use a clamp (a G-cramp, if possible) to ensure that the veneer remains flat while the glue is drying. Place a piece of paper over the repaired blister to stop the glue sticking to the clamp. Thin pieces of timber between the paper and the cramp heads protect the surface from bruising. If the blister is in the centre of* *a panel, and cannot be clamped, press it with a hot iron until the surface is completely flat. Again, a piece of paper between the iron and the blister keeps the iron free of glue. Use the tips of your fingers to check for any further bumps.*

▲ **4** *If a syringe is not available, insert the glue using the point of a scalpel. Spread the glue under the veneer, making sure that the blistered area is completely covered. Keep a scalpel or knife* *especially for this purpose – glue is difficult to remove from the blade and will make it blunt.*

MEMO

Tools and materials
Craft knife, scalpel or veneer knife

PVA glue

Cast-iron iron or electric iron

Hypodermic syringe

Weights or cramps

Paper

Precautions
Keep glue off veneered surface whenever possible.

Check that glue does not react adversely with veneer by testing on an inconspicuous part.

Common problems
Too much heat will loosen undamaged veneer.

Appropriate surfaces
Cutting with a knife is best on straight-grained veneers. The cut line is less likely to be seen afterwards on figured veneers and on veneers with interlocking grain.

Drying time
Only use the iron for about 30 seconds.

29

Repairing veneers

SEE ALSO

28–29
DEALING WITH
BLISTERS

40–43
HOW TO USE
STOPPERS

There are times when veneers need to be repaired, which probably means letting in a piece of matching veneer, unless the damaged section can be used again. The important thing is to choose a good match and cut it correctly, so that the grain runs easily from old to new, with no join showing.

Remember when choosing a veneer patch that grain is as important as colour for a good match. Also remember that, if the workpiece has not been stripped back, the patch must start lighter in colour than the surrounding veneer, as the finish you intend to apply will darken it.

The most common veneer faults are along the edges of drawers or table tops, often where the cross-banding has been detached. For these repairs it is sometimes best to remove whole strips of veneer and replace them completely, rather than attempt a match. Specialist veneer and marquetry outlets sell a wide selection of cross-bandings and inlays and stock small quantities of veneer for repair work. If you know what veneer you need, these outlets will mail you the relevant items.

How to repair veneer

The most essential tool for repairing veneers is a sharp knife. When cutting out faults, try to follow the grain or cut at a tangent to it. Where possible, cut a wavy line – as the eye is less likely to be drawn towards such a repair, especially on the more figured veneers. As a result, repairs are generally easiest to disguise on those complex woods.

If you have a number of repairs to make, veneer punches are especially useful. They are designed to cut out the fault from the damaged veneer and a matching patch from the new material. Veneer punches are made in a variety of sizes and have irregular cutters to help disguise the repair.

Once a cut has been made around the fault, remove the offending piece, taking care not to damage the surrounding veneer. Also take great care choosing the orientation of the patch, marking it to ensure the fit is correct when you come to glue it down with PVA glue. Once it is in place, use an iron to flatten the repair in much the same way as a blister (see pages 28–29).

**Repairing
damaged veneer**
▶ **1** *The corner of this panel has been damaged and the veneer needs to be repaired. The usual remedies for surface faults, stoppers and fillers, are unlikely to hold on a corner like* *this, and colour matching would be difficult. The best solution is to let in a new piece of matching veneer.*

◀ **2** *Trim off the rough edge of damaged veneer using a craft knife and a straightedge. This ensures a neat join. Cut cleanly and firmly, with the straightedge covering the undamaged veneer, so that if there is a slip, the knife will score only the piece to be removed. Use one very light cut to mark the line, and then slice through the veneer in a single stroke. Try not to cut into the groundwork.*

MEMO

❖

Tools and materials

Veneer to suit

PVA glue

Veneer knife

Electric iron

Veneer or masking tape

Veneer punch

❖

Common problems

Cutting straight across the grain makes a more obvious repair.

Novice repairers tend not to cut close enough to the shape.

◀ **3** *Remove all loose pieces of veneer. It is possible that the groundwork has also been damaged, and that pieces have come loose. If this has happened, glue any chips back in place and fill any cavities, ensuring that the surface is flat.*

▼ **5** *Select a piece of veneer for the repair. Try to find a piece that matches the original both in colour and grain pattern. Cut it so that the grain follows that of the panel. It is best to cut a slightly larger piece than necessary, and trim it down after the glue has dried. Try to let in the new piece of veneer at an angle of about 30 degrees to the grain.*

▲ **4** *Apply glue liberally to the area to be repaired. Use PVA glue for this. Spread the glue over the area, making sure that there is enough to be squeezed out by the new piece of veneer.*

HINTS AND TIPS

• When using delicate veneers, tape the face with veneer or masking tape before cutting out the new patch. Mark the tape so you can position the patch.

• Try to hit a veneer punch with only one hammer blow in order to achieve a clean cut. Similarly, cut through the veneer as cleanly as possible when using a knife.

• Sharpen the outside of veneer punches to keep them very sharp.

◄ 6 *Use a hot iron to speed up the bonding of the glue. Place a piece of paper between the veneer and the iron to avoid marking. Press down hard with the iron for about a minute, and then check to see if the glue has dried.*

◄ 7 *Once the glue has dried, trim off any excess veneer. Take off the bulk of the surplus with a sharp knife, and then use a rasp or file, drawing it downwards only.*

Types of veneer

▼ *Keep a store of veneers in a variety of colours and grain patterns. You may have to play around with your veneers to find a piece that matches, but do try to use a matching timber species – different timbers all change colour with time. Shown here a range of*

exotic and more commonplace veneers:
1 *Bird's-eye maple*
2 *Plane tree*
3 *Castello*
4 *Rosewood, santos*
5 *European walnut*
6 *Ash*
7 *Padauk*

► 8 *Sand down the inserted veneer, using 100 grade garnet paper folded around a cork block. Keep the block flat and sand along the direction of the grain.*

► 9 *The panel is now flat and smooth, and the repair is indiscernible from the rest. The colour will change once a finish has been applied to the repair, and colours can be used later to improve the colour match.*

Stains in the wood

B lue and iron stains are faults within the wood that occur during the kiln drying done by the timber merchant or sawmill. Blue stain is caused by a mould, which grows on timber and leaves blue marks that look like ink stains.

Iron stain is caused by particles of iron from nails, screws, saw blades, corrugated-iron roofs and even shrapnel, which react with tannic acid present in the timber. Oak is renowned for reacting in this way. The stains, which appear as black flecks in the grain, usually show up after sanding.

MEMO

❖

Safety precautions
Always wear protective gloves, goggles and protection over clothing when using bleach. Only use bleach in a well-ventilated room or outdoors.

Follow manufacturer's instructions carefully and thoroughly.

Always have plenty of water available in case of spillage.

Wear a mask when sanding surfaces after bleaching.

Always pour oxalic crystals into water – never pour the water onto the crystals.

❖

Tools and materials
Protective gloves and goggles

Oxalic acid crystals (or two-part bleach for large or deep stains)

Water and hosepipe

Grass brush

Mask

Glass, plastic, enamel or earthenware container

▼ **2** *Oxalic acid is supplied as a white powder in dry crystal form. Remember that it is poisonous. Always wear protective gloves, and ensure that your hands are washed after working. Use glass, plastic or earthenware containers for mixing and storing the crystals.*

Removing stains
▲ **1** *Iron stains are particularly common in oak. They are caused by tannic acid in the timber reacting with iron filings implanted in the grain.*

This dark stain must be bleached using oxalic acid before the piece can be finished.

33

Cleaning stains

To remove stains, use a bleach (preferably oxalic acid crystals) that is neither too strong nor too weak. A two-part bleach (see pages 50–52) may be too powerful for small isolated patches. Instead, unless the stains are large or stubborn slowly add oxalic crystals to warm water making up to a saturated solution (see pages 50–52). About a cupful of solution is needed to bleach a table top.

Apply the bleach solution with a grass brush (see pages 14–15). It is best not to saturate the timber with bleach, as adhesives may be affected. Leave the workpiece to dry, and repeat the process if the stain is persistent. Once the stain has disappeared, you must neutralize the surface with plenty of clean water. Finally, leave the piece to dry.

▲ **3** *Make a saturated acid solution by adding the crystals to warm water and stirring. Keep adding crystals until no more will dissolve.*

Always add the crystals to the water, and not the other way round. Leave to stand for about 10 minutes before use.

▶ **4** *Apply the oxalic acid with a grass brush. The bristles of a normal brush are likely to fall out when used with bleach. Lay on the bleach evenly over the stain. Do not splash it around, and always wear goggles. Try not to let droplets fall on the surface where they will mark the piece.*

◀ **5** *After applying the bleach, leave it to soak into the timber for about half an hour, until dry. More stubborn stains may need further applications of bleach before they are completely removed.*

Avoid saturating veneered surfaces – the glue bond may be weakened by the water-based solution.

HINTS AND TIPS

- Work outside.
- Keep a hosepipe ready.
- When working on a large area, such as a table top, use a cleat under the board to prohibit any tendency to bow when dampened.

◀ **6** *Wash the surface with plenty of clean water.*

▶ **7** *Once the wood has dried there should be no evidence of stain or bleaching. Sand the surface lightly with fine 240 grit garnet.*

Chemical stripping

WORKING WITH CHEMICAL STRIPPERS

● When using strippers that make the finish bubble, dab on a second coat of stripper to flatten and burst the blisters in order to bring the stripper into contact with the surface again.

● Leave stripper on the surface for at least 15 minutes before removing it.

● It does not help to "paint" the stripper onto the surface – it is better to lay down the first coat, and dab on subsequent coats.

The removal of old finishes can be a laborious task, but must be carried out properly if subsequent finishing is to be a success. It is essential to clean any evidence of previous decoration or protection from the grain. Otherwise, it will show up later – and all the effort of stripping and finishing will have been wasted.

Using cabinet scrapers or sanders is an alternative to chemical stripping, but is much more time-consuming and unlikely to produce a better result. In addition, sanding or scraping removes the patina that certain woods such as mahogany acquire on ageing. Sanding will also not remove the residue of finish from open-grained woods. It is often better to use a solvent paint remover (see below).

Abrasives may also be used for stripping, but they can cut through the fibres of the wood and there is always a chance of an uneven finish, with some areas sanded back more deeply than others.

A further alternative is to take the piece to a specialist who has access to sandblasting facilities or a caustic dipping tank. Unfortunately, this latter technique often loosens joints in furniture and doors. Sandblasting works well for intricate pieces and carving; it needs no neutralizing and usually leaves the wood ready for refinishing.

When doing the work oneself, the choice of stripper is determined by the workpiece and the original finish. It is of course easy to distinguish paint from wax, but other finishes are more difficult to identify. The best way to test a finish is to try a solvent on a less prominent part of the work, for example, inside rails on a chair.

Stripping old finishes
◀ 1 *Decant the stripper carefully into a paint kettle. Apply it to the piece with a flat brush. Always wear protective PVC gloves, goggles and protective clothing when working with chemical strippers. Take care when opening cans of stripper – pressure can build up and force the liquid to spurt out into your eyes.*

◀ **2** *Allow the stripper to soak into the old finish. Make sure that enough is applied to keep the surface wet. Do not spread the stripper – this will cause it to evaporate too quickly.*

▶ **3** *Test with a scraper to see if the finish has dissolved and is ready for scraping. Do not try to scrape the surface too soon – the job will be easier if you wait for the stripper to take effect fully. Use a paint scraper to remove the waste, working along the grain. The old finish is soaked in stripper, so roll it up in newspaper and make sure it is discarded out of harm's way.*

◀ **4** *Having cleaned the surface with a scraper, apply a further coat of stripper, wait for a few minutes and then rub off using coarse wire wool (3 or 4 grade). Wire wool is very sharp. Use a pair of old scissors to cut it, and always wear protective gloves. Rub the remaining finish away, working into every nook and cranny, leaving the surface clean.*

MEMO

❖

Safety precautions
Wear PVC gloves and goggles at all times when using strippers.

Wash strippers off skin immediately with water.

Only use strippers outdoors or in well-ventilated areas. Do not use them in a confined space.

Solvents can cause dizziness.

Scrape off residue onto an old newspaper for disposal.

Some strippers are flammable, so do not smoke or light a naked flame near them.

Make sure all stripper is removed before handling the workpiece.

Make sure the stripper is removed from all nooks and crannies, corners and covings. Otherwise, it will react with stains and finishes.

Always ensure that the surface has been either neutralized or wiped with white spirit, whichever is appropriate, before refinishing.

Tools and materials
Gloves and goggles

Chemical stripper

Wire wool

Brush

White spirit

Cabinet scraper or paint scraper

◄ 5 Once the piece has been cleaned, check on the label to see if the product needs neutralizing. It is often sufficient to wipe the surface with a rag and white spirit. To neutralize an acid-based stripper make up a solution of washing soda and water. Mix 2 cups of soda with 4.5l (1 gall) of hot water.

▲ 6 Swab the surface with the soda solution on a rag, washing away any residue, and making *sure all the corners and less accessible parts are treated. Any stripper that is left in or on the* *wood will react with later finishes.*

USING WIRE WOOL

- There is a range of wire wool grades, the finest usually being referred to as 0000

- Do not try to pull pieces of coarse wire wool from a roll, as the strands of metal are sharp and can easily cut your hands and fingers.

- Cut wire wool with old or cheap scissors.

- Use wire wool in wads about fist-size.

- When clogged with wax or dirt, turn wire wool inside out to make full use of it. Large wads are very wasteful.

- The finest wire wool burnishes the surface when used with some modern finishes, instead of dulling it.

White spirit

To clean wax or grime from a workpiece without harming other finishes, use white spirit on a rag. If nothing seems to happen, rub with fine wire wool instead of rag, using small wads about the size of a golf ball. Replace the wad when it is clogged with wax and dirt, cutting it off the roll with scissors.

Solvent strippers

Solvent strippers are supplied ready-mixed. They contain a mixture of solvents, usually methylene chloride, with some wax to stop them evaporating, and are used to remove French polish, cellulose-based finishes, oil and wax. To apply, simply lay the stripper onto the surface, using a flat brush. Do not move the stripper around once on the workpiece, as that is likely to hasten evaporation.

Leave the stripper to soak into the finish, keeping the surface wet. You will then be able to remove the finish with a paint or cabinet scraper. Always scrape in the direction of the grain (if the direction isn't obvious, remove a small area of finish from an inconspicuous part to check which way the grain runs). It may be necessary to apply several coats of stripper before the bulk of the old coating is removed.

Once most of the original coating has been cut back, use wire wool to pick up the last flecks of finish. This is particularly useful for mouldings, nooks and crannies, and timber with a deep and open grain structure. Before further work on the surface, some solvent strippers need to be neutralized. Always check on the product's label. To neutralize an acid-based stripper apply a wash of water and soda and leave to dry. The water will raise the grain and the wood will

◄ **7** *If the piece is very badly scratched or dented, sand with progressively finer abrasive paper, starting with 100 grit and working up to 240. However, bear in mind that certain woods acquire a beautiful patina on ageing which sanding would remove. Check the surface thoroughly for any remnants of finish, or any bruises and dents before starting the next stages of restoration.*

then need to be sanded down before refinishing takes place. To neutralize an alkaline stripper use acetic acid.

Unless a manufacturer specifically states that a product needs neutralizing, it is usually sufficient to wipe the surface with a rag dipped in white spirit. This does not raise the grain.

Be warned that solvent strippers in paste form contain caustic soda and will cause many woods to darken.

▶ **8** *Stripping can reveal many problems formerly concealed under years of paint. Some of the joints may be loose, and the piece may need some filling, but otherwise it is ready for finishing.*

How to use stoppers

Stoppers are used for filling larger indentations in wood, in much the same way as plaster fillers are used for making good dents and cracks in plasterwork. The main difference is that stoppers have to match the colour of the piece, and require an elastic nature to cope with the movement of timber. It is best to avoid using stoppers, if at all possible, because a good match is always difficult. However, for cracks, knots and deep scratches there is often no alternative.

Select the best stopper for the situation. When choosing a stopper, it is important to bear in mind the type of finish you intend to use on the piece. While shellac sticks are suitable for any finish, plastic wood (in either two-part or one-part form) is a difficult material to match. If you intend to use a stain to do so, make sure it is compatible. The instructions will say whether it is oil or water based.

As a general rule use shellac stoppers under traditional finishes, and two-part stoppers under modern spray finishes. Only use wax stoppers for small chips, and then only while polishing, or with a wax or oil finish. Plastic wood is most commonly used under varnishes.

Although some stoppers will take a stain once dry, a more successful technique is to mix pigment with the stopper before applying.

Shellac sticks

Shellac sticks are sold in a variety of colours to suit a range of woods, and are a concentrated form of the shellac used for French polishing. They are available from only a few specialist DIY stores and by mail order (see "Useful Addresses" in the back of this book).

Select a good colour match and hold the shellac stick over the affected area. Using a soldering iron or hot knife, melt the shellac into the fault, melting enough to leave the stopper proud after pushing it well into the hole.

Shellac stopping should not be used under two-part cold-cure lacquers.

Plastic wood

This is a common stopper, available from most hardware and DIY shops. It comes in a tin and is made in a range of colours. Plastic wood dries out quickly, so remember to replace the lid immediately after use.

Plastic wood does not always adhere effectively, so make sure any faults are clean and free from dust. Apply with a knife or chisel, pressing the stopper well into the cavity. Plastic wood has a tendency to shrink, so leave proud to dry. It may even be necessary to use more than one application; for large holes, fill gradually.

Filling with stopper
▲ **1** *Stopper is used as a filling when pieces of a finish have chipped away. For this picture frame, shellac stick stopper has been used. Shellac sticks are available from specialist suppliers.*

◀ **2** *Mask the area around the fault with masking tape to protect the original finish.*

▲ **3** *Hold a soldering iron just above the surface of the piece, and press the shellac stick against it so that it melts* *and drops into the fault like sealing wax. Build up the stopper gradually.*

▲ **5** *Leave the stopper to set for about 5 minutes. Once it is set it may be necessary to level it with a small chisel. Do not* *try to take too much stopper off at a time – it is brittle and likely to break up if too much pressure is used.*

▲ **4** *Level the stopper with a steel scraper or other tool before it sets. It is important to manipulate the stopper* *to follow the contours of the surface as closely as possible. Do not overfill the hole, but do leave the stopper slightly proud.*

▲ **6** *Use coarse abrasive paper for final levelling. On flat surfaces sand with a sanding block, but on mouldings just fold the 100 garnet paper and delicately* *work with the corners. Do not over-sand, creating a hollow. When it is smooth, finish with fine abrasive.*

Mixing glue and sawdust

▲ **1** *A quick and cheap stopper can be made by mixing glue with sawdust to match the workpiece. Mix PVA adhesive with the appropriate sawdust on a piece of card. Add the sawdust to the glue until it has a thick but workable consistency, for large holes. Make sure the glue is thoroughly mixed in for a good bond.*

▲ **2** *Use dry pigments to achieve the desired colour, mixing them gradually into the glue and sawdust stopper. Always mix enough to fill the hole – the exact colour may be difficult to repeat.*

▶ **3** *Apply the stopper with a plastic or card spatula. Spread it over the fault, building up to the surface until it is smooth but a little proud.*

▶ **4** *Glue and sawdust stopper must be left for at least two or three hours to dry. It will then be stuck firmly into the hole, and hard enough to be shaped and smoothed with files and abrasives.*

Two-part stoppers

Two-part stoppers are harder versions of plastic wood. A catalyst or hardener reacts with the stopper to create a very strong repair. They are available in a variety of colours, and can be matched using stains and pigments (see pages 44–49). But achieving an exact match can be difficult, so they are better used for structural repairs (especially on particle board) than for filling conspicuous faults.

Follow the instructions carefully, applying the filler with a knife or chisel and leaving it slightly proud. These two-part stoppers do shrink, but not to the extent of plastic wood, and they set very hard – so beware of over-filling, which will necessitate time-consuming chiselling and sanding later.

Water-based wood stoppers

As their name suggests, water-based wood stoppers can be thinned with water. They have the advantage of being quick-drying and suffer very little shrinkage. They are available in a wide range of colours and are cheaper than two-part stoppers.

Glue and sawdust mix

A quick and cheap stopper can be made by mixing glue with sawdust to match the workpiece. It is not a good filler for large areas, and not all finishes take to it, but it works well for gaps along joint lines.

When using PVA adhesive, mix with sawdust produced by sanding either the piece to be repaired or an offcut of the original timber. As PVA will not fill gaps, plenty of wood dust is needed to act as a filler. Alternatively, for larger holes, use a urea-formaldehyde adhesive mixed with sawdust.

Leave all these mixtures slightly proud, then chisel and sand them flat when dry. These homemade stoppers are all water-based and take stain fairly well once dry – but it's best to mix in the stain and experiment with colour before application.

Wax sticks

Manufacturers of wax finishes also make sticks for small repairs. These are coloured and designed for use either on surfaces to be waxed or on pieces already polished. Clear beeswax may be sufficient in many circumstances, especially when the hole is small. However, wax must not be used under modern finishes. Use wax sticks like shellac sticks, warming the wax with a soldering iron. Push the wax into the holes or chips with a small filling knife, then scrape off any excess with a chisel or scraper once hard.

Using pigments to colour two-part stopper

▲ **1** *Having sanded the stopper smooth and level, use pigments to match the repair with the rest of the surface of the piece. Pigments are opaque colours, which are ground into a binding medium which can be oil, acrylic, alkid or shellac.*

▶ **2** *Use the pigments to mask out the defect. A selection of nine colours is sufficient, stored in a tray. Experiment with combinations of pigments to judge the colour matches they produce.*

▶ **3** *Mix the pigments with shellac polish and apply with a pencil brush. Dip the brush into pale polish, and then into the required pigment, and mix. Here titanium white and yellow ochre are being mixed to produce a light colour.*

▶ **4** *Apply the mixture of pigment and polish with a No. 6 pencil brush, stroking on the colour and imitating the grain pattern. Blend in the colour gradually.*

▲ **5** *Leave to dry for 2–3 minutes. Gradually apply polish over the stopper to bring out the colour. Too much polish at a time will rub off the colour.*

Staining wood

SEE ALSO

73-75
WAXED FINISHES

124-149
SPRAY FINISHES

Stains consist of dyes dissolved in a medium and are used for colouring timber. They do so by soaking into the grain of the wood, giving it a tint – unlike pigments used for colouring paint, which lie on top of the surface as solid matter.

The medium carrying the dye determines the characteristics of the stain, such as drying time, compatibility and spread. A stain should enhance the grain and improve the appearance of the wood; it needs to be easy to apply, has to be compatible with the finish, and should dry within a reasonable time. It should also maintain its colour, without fading. Stains are particularly good at upgrading timber and making unattractive surfaces more interesting.

Although most wood stains are designed to soak into the timber, for exterior work the stain forms a film on the surface, creating an effect similar to paint. Nevertheless, most stains do not offer protection and so need further finishing.

When choosing a stain, select the one that has the most suitable characteristics. The same colour can be produced using different types of stain. Colour is therefore not the only criterion for selection. Rather, your choice should be determined by a number of important considerations, which you need to keep in mind when investigating the various options. For example: how fast do you want the stain to dry? What finish and timber do you want to use the stain with? Will the stained piece be affected by wear and tear? Does the stain have to match an original antique colour?

What are water stains?

Water stains are supplied in a dry powder or crystal form and then dissolved in water. They have been used for hundreds of years, originally being made with vegetable dyes obtained from trees and plants. They are now the cheapest of all stains and can be bought by mail order from finishing specialists. Although the original dyes are no longer available, the manmade alternatives are useful to have around the workshop.

The most useful dyes are Vandyke crystals (brown), mahogany crystals (warm brown), and nigrosine (black). You can mix these dyes in order to produce different colours. By changing the ratio of water to powder, you can adjust the depth of colour. Always test water stains on an offcut before applying them. Also check the effect of adding a finish.

**A selection of
different stains to
show colour range**
◄ *Substrate: Red oak.*
1 *Yellow.*
2 *Blue-black.*
3 *Golden oak.*
4 *Light oak.*
5 *Olive.*
6 *Rosewood.*

Working with water stains

Apply the stain with a rag, brush or wadding. You can use any of these methods – but you will find that a brush is best for mouldings, corners and carvings, and that wadding holds the most stain. Wet the wood before applying the first coat of stain, to aid an even spread. Rub the stain into the grain, keeping a wet edge all the time.

For a table top you will need about a cupful of stain, but make sure you have enough for the whole piece. Use plenty of stain, only stopping short of pouring it onto the surface. Water stains dry slowly, so you will have time to wipe off the excess with a cloth or absorbent paper. Once the stain has dried, go over any light areas with another coat.

Using water stains
▶ **1** *Water stains are supplied in powder form. Make up the stain by adding the powder to water in different proportions depending on the colour required. Add more stain to make it darker, and more water to make it lighter.*

HINTS FOR STAINING

● Although stains dry lighter, they are darkened by subsequent finishes – so test the effect on an offcut or hidden area first.

● You can always make a surface darker with more stain, but it is impossible to lighten the colour without resorting to bleach.

● A dark stain has a stronger effect on a light wood than on a dark one.

● Always keep a wet edge when applying stain, to avoid patchy colour.

● Plan your staining pattern before starting, so you maintain a uniform colour.

● If the workpiece is dampened very slightly with water, that will give some idea of the colour effects of applying a clear finish before or after staining.

● When trying to match colours, do so gradually. Don't attempt to mix the perfect combination of dyes straight off – rather, use progressive coats of individual dyes.

▼ **2** *Stir the solution thoroughly to ensure the powder has dissolved. Keep one spatula for stirring and another for picking up powder. Hot water and a few drops of ammonia added to the solution can improve the stain's penetration. Leave for 10 minutes before use.*

45

What are solvent wood dyes?

These dyes are supplied ready-mixed, usually in tins, the dyes being dissolved in white spirit, naphtha or a similar hydrocarbon solvent. They are classified by wood colour, with names such as "dark mahogany" or "light oak". However, all these dyes can be used on any timber, and the names are no more than general guides. Solvent wood dyes are most commonly used on joinery and are the stains most widely stocked by DIY stores.

Select the wood dye closest to the colour required, and build it up to produce the desired shade. If the colour is too dark, it can be thinned with the appropriate solvent.

Working with solvent wood dyes

Solvent wood dyes do not raise the grain, but they do bite into deep and uneven grain (as occurs in beech), which may show up as dark patches. It is therefore important to prepare rough areas especially carefully. Wood dyes are convenient to use and penetrate deeply into the timber. They are useful for working outdoors, since water stains take a long time to dry and spirit stains dry too quickly for large areas to be stained.

▼ 3 Apply the stain with rag or wadding. Use plenty of stain, keeping it wet on the surface all the time, to produce an even spread. Rub it in with a circular motion. Use a brush for staining mouldings, but as with a flat surface always keep a wet edge.

▲ 4 Water stain dries slowly so you will have plenty of time to wipe off any excess. Do this with wadding or rag, following the grain. Leave to dry for about an hour before continuing the finishing process.

▼ 5 The stain may well dry lighter, as is the case with most finishes. It will also feel rough where the water has raised the grain, so use 240 grade fine abrasive to lightly sand the surface. Work with the grain, sanding very gently so as not to sand through the colour, especially on the corners.

PROBLEMS WHEN STAINING

- Faults and end grain often absorb great quantities of stain, which makes them look darker. You may therefore need to seal them with a shellac sealer before staining.

- Avoid stain runs by working on the underside of a piece first.

- It is not possible to create a "rosewood" effect with a single stain. The only way is to apply a mahogany stain – then, when dry, add black streaks with ebony stain, using a pencil brush.

- Because of the absorption differences with the grain, it is sometimes better to use a varnish stain (see pages 76-79) for pine.

What are spirit stains?

These stains are aniline dyes dissolved in methylated spirits or alcohol. Professional woodworkers like using them because of the wide range of colours available.

Dyes are named by their colour (for example, spirit yellow and spirit green), except for Bismarck brown which, confusingly, is nearer red. They can be applied by brush, cloth or spray gun and are also used for dipping work. Because of the spirit base, they can be mixed with shellac polish for colour matching and touching up during the polishing process.

Spirit stains dry very fast. As a result, they are ideal for spraying. Also, the wood is ready for coating almost immediately. However, the fact that they dry so quickly makes them difficult to apply successfully and can result in a patchy finish. Use spirit stains for items such as toys that are small enough to be dipped in a small dipping tank or container.

One disadvantage of a spirit base is that if coats of shellac are applied later, they are likely to lift the stain and affect the colour.

Working with spirit stains

Spirit stains are sold in powder form, as aniline dyes, and mixed to the desired colour – more powder being used to provide a darker shade. The dyes can be mixed together for a wider range of colours. Apply the stain sparingly, or the dye will be removed by the polish. When dipping, leave the item in the tank for about 5 minutes.

It is a good idea to add a small quantity of transparent French polish to the formulation to "fix" the spirit stain on the wood.

What are chemical stains?

Chemical stains have been used for hundreds of years and can produce many different effects – some attractive, some less so. Strictly speaking, they are not stains in the true sense. Most of them are colourless, and they do not stain the wood but change its colour when they are applied. This colour change is brought about by the "stains" reacting with chemicals present in the timber. As the chemicals in timber differ from one piece to another, the colour can vary (the chemical structure of the timber depends on the climate and location of the tree during growth). The best-known of these chemicals is probably tannic acid, which occurs in oak. These chemicals are difficult to get hold of in DIY shops. However they are available direct from suppliers by mail order (see the list of "Useful Addresses" in the back of the book).

The main chemicals used for staining are listed below:

- Ammonia (as a 10 per cent solution in water to darken timber)
- Bichromate of potash
- Sulphate of iron (green copperas)
- Permanganate of potash

Working with chemical stains

Dissolve the chemical powder in water, creating a saturated solution, as with water stains. Warm water helps to dissolve the chemicals faster. About 2 teaspoons of bichromate of potash to 1 pint of water is a standard solution for mahogany. Apply with a brush, wiping off the surplus, then leave the "stain" to work. Once the desired colour has been achieved, neutralize the chemicals with methylated spirits. Don't use bichromate of potash under a two-part cold cure acid catalysed lacquer, as this can result in a fault known as pinholing, where the surface is pitted with tiny holes.

After using chemical stains wash all containers thoroughly to remove all trace of chemicals.

Sealing inlay before staining
▼ **1** *The contrast in colour between different inlays may be lost when a piece is stained. To prevent this, apply white or transparent polish to seal an inlay before staining.*

What are pigment-suspension stains?

This range of finishes is made from finely ground pigments, suspended in a medium. The pigments do not dissolve, as dyes do – because they are ground so fine, they are not heavy enough to sink and are, instead,

continually suspended in the medium.

Pigment-suspension stains give a semi-opaque colour to timber. They are useful for improving low-grade wood, producing greater tone and making the piece more attractive.

Working with pigment-suspension stains

When supplied in powder form, pigment-suspension stains are mixed with water to the required colour. Use about 1 teaspoon of powder to every pint of water for a standard stain. They are also available in a ready-mixed

▶ **3** *Once the sealer is dry, apply the stain over the whole panel. Use a water or solvent wood dye, but not a spirit stain. Methylated spirits would dissolve the polish and ruin the seal. Rub in the stain evenly, applying it wet in circular motions and then straightening up along the grain. Leave to dry.*

▼ **4** *After the stain has dried, the outer, sealed inlay has retained its natural pale yellow colour. However, the* inner string has absorbed the stain, and has turned a light brown.

▶ **2** *On this rosewood panel with boxwood stringing, the outer inlay is to be sealed, but the thinner, inner one is not. Pick out the inlay carefully so that no part of it is missed, using a No. 6 pencil brush, and be sure to keep to the line. Leave to dry for 15 minutes.*

range of colours. Apply pigment-suspension stains generously with a brush or cloth. Be sure to remove surplus stain, otherwise the colour may look patchy and opaque.

What are wax stains?

Wax stains are supplied in soft wax form, ready-made in various colours, and are used directly on the timber or over existing stain. Wax stains cannot

be used under finishes such as polyurethane or two-part cold-cure lacquers. They are useful for burnishing mouldings, carvings and turned wood.

Working with wax stains

Apply wax stains with a cloth, like a wax polish, rubbing the wax into the timber. Leave the surface to dry, preferably overnight, before buffing.

Making a paper boat
Boats are traditionally used for mixing and holding small quantities of finish. They are a useful way of using up old sandpaper, and can be disposed of after use.

1 *Take a piece of sandpaper (7.5 × 12.5cm; 3 × 5in).*

2 *Fold in the two long ends.*

3 *Fold in the two short ends.*

4 *Open out to show folds.*

5 *Fold corners together.*

6 *Fold long ends over to hold in shape.*

7 *Fold over ends to form rim.*

8 *Both ends folded over holding the container square.*

MEMO

CHEMICAL STAINS
Tools and materials
Chemical powder

Water

Brush

Glass, plastic or earthenware container

Safety precautions
Always wear gloves and goggles.

Drying time
Allow to work until the desired effect is achieved.

PIGMENT-SUSPENSION STAINS
Tools and materials
Brush or cloth

Powder or ready-mixed stain

Drying time
About 1 hour.

WAX STAINS
Tools and materials
Soft cloth

Fine wire wool

Wax stain

Drying time
Leave overnight.

Bleaching wood

Bleaches are used to lighten the colour of timber. This may be desirable for purely aesthetic reasons, as a matter of taste, on new materials or older darkened timber; or to remove blemishes and stains; or to make darker components compatible with other parts of a piece. Bleaching may be needed to tone down the colour of stripped wood, and is also used to remove ink marks and water marks (see pages 33-35).

There are many different types of bleach, and the household variety can be used on timber; but the best approach is either to mix your own, using oxalic acid with water, or to buy a special bleach for timber (sold in a two-part pack) that generates a stronger reaction with the surface. For the latter product a neutralizer is essential, in order to halt the chemical reaction and ensure that any residue of bleach does not harm further finishes. A 5 per cent solution of acetic acid in water is the traditional way to neutralize two-part bleach, with plenty of water to clean the surface.

Since bleaches are likely to react with metal (they are used to reverse the effects of iron filings on timber), always use glass, plastic or earthenware containers when working with these chemicals. They are dangerous substances, so read the manufacturer's instructions carefully and follow the safety advice given. Always keep bleaches away from children; and never store or use in food containers, in case they are mistakenly eaten or drunk.

Using two-part bleaches

▲ **1** *Bleaching will bring down the tone of the colour of this piece and remove the marks.*

▲ **2** *Apply the contents of pack A or 1 with a brush, keeping both the container and brush clearly marked to avoid confusion between this and pack B or 2. Always wear heavy protective* *gloves, and apply the chemical thoroughly so that the piece has an even coat.*

▶ **3** *Five minutes after coating the surface with the first application, apply the contents of pack B or 2, also with a brush, and also wearing gloves. The surface will look darker at this stage. The reaction of the two chemicals lightens the wood, and sometimes this will produce a foam. Leave the piece until the desired effect is achieved.*

◀ **4** *Once the required colour has been achieved the reaction must be neutralized. Use a 5 per cent solution of acetic acid and water, applied with a brush.*

▼ **5** *Rub the acetic acid solution into the grain to neutralize all the bleach, otherwise the result will be patchy. Leave to dry.*

◀ **6** *The bleached item.*

51

Oxalic-acid bleach

Oxalic-acid crystals, as supplied by chemists and finishing suppliers, are mixed with water to a saturated solution to produce a weak bleach. They are adequate for removing stains and marks on most timbers, but not really strong enough for changing the colour of large surfaces. Oxalic acid is cheap and the crystals are easy to mix, using 450g (1lb) crystals to 4.5l (1 gall) water. The water does not have to be warm, but warm water does help to dissolve oxalic acid. Always measure the water into the container (which must not be metal) first, and then pour in the crystals.

Apply evenly and wet using a grass brush (see pages 14-15), following the grain, then leave to dry. If the colour has not lightened sufficiently, apply the bleach again and leave. Once the desired effect is achieved, wash thoroughly with plenty of clean water. The bleach will have done most of its work within half an hour. More will be needed for further change.

Oxalic acid can also be used for cleaning off dirt from old timber, especially oak, and for degreasing oily surfaces such as teak.

Two-part bleaches

These bleaches are powerful lightening agents and can change wood to a much lighter shade. They are also dangerous, so take care with both storage and use.

The bleaches are supplied in two plastic bottles, normally labelled A and B or 1 and 2. The first bottle contains a solution, which may darken the timber; by adding the peroxide solution in the second bottle the bleaching action is sparked off. It is important to check which bottle is which and they must be kept separate, as mixing them causes a violent reaction and they can even explode.

Apply the contents of the first bottle (A or 1), using a grass brush, and leave for 5 minutes before applying the contents of the second bottle. Use equal quantities of each part, without drenching the timber. They will foam on the surface, and bleach the wood by oxidizing. Leave until dry, or until the required effect is achieved. Then the bleach must be neutralized with water and acetic acid.

Household bleach

Household bleach is applied like an oxalic-acid solution, but it only has a limited effect and is most useful for removing marks. Leave it to dry and then wash down with water.

EASY TO BLEACH	TWO APPLICATIONS NECESSARY	HARD TO BLEACH
Ash	Mahogany	Cherry
Elm	Oak	Rosewood
Beech	Walnut	Satinwood
Sycamore	Western red cedar	Padauk
Birch	Eucalyptus	Ebony
Pear	Chestnut	Wenge
Apple	Yew	Black walnut
Hemlock	Douglas fir	Jacaranda

Grain fillers

SEE ALSO

20-22
ABRASIVES

44-49
STAINING WOOD

Some timbers, such as oak, have an open grain structure that makes the perfectly smooth finish characteristic of French polishing hard to achieve. With these timbers, the open pores need to be filled with a fine powder applied as a paste or liquid. This choking of the grain also makes polishing quicker, as the grain does not have to be filled with polish – which is the alternative time-consuming solution.

Originally grain fillers were made of plaster of Paris mixed with water and a pigment, but these plaster fillers tended to turn white and show up in the grain. Modern grain fillers are therefore made from a mixture of filling powder, binder, pigment and solvent. There are many variations on this theme, each recommended for specific tasks, the distinguishing feature being the type of binder used.

Fillers are sold by weight and in a variety of colours. A selection of mahogany, walnut and light oak is sufficient to start with. Solvent wood dyes can be mixed with white-spirit-based fillers, but generally grain fillers are difficult to colour as they require pigments that have to be ground into the binder.

Use hessian or a coarse cloth to apply grain fillers, rubbing them into the grain in a circular motion. Don't work the filler in the direction of the grain, or the filler may not hold in the pores. Wipe off excess filler across the grain with a piece of hessian. If a white-spirit-based filler has been used, then wipe off across the grain with a piece of rag dampened with white spirit to remove any filler sitting on the surface. Leave other fillers to dry, then lightly rub with fine abrasive paper to remove any small particles of filler that may remain on the surface.

WHICH FILLER TO USE

Oil-bound fillers
Oil-bound fillers are often called patent fillers. They are not recommended for use with nitrocellulose finishes, but can be applied before a polyurethane or shellac polish. They are easy to use and are supplied ready-mixed.

Resin-bound fillers
Resin fillers are sold ready-mixed as a paste in a range of colours. Pigments have to be ground into fillers to ensure they are fully absorbed into the resin, so it is better to use the colours as sold. Resin fillers can take any finish, are easy to wipe off, and are good for oily timbers.

Two-pack fillers
These fillers have to be used with a hardener, or catalyst, and are supplied in tins. The correct ratio is usually 3 parts filler to 1 part catalyst. The filler is coloured, and like others can be bought in a range of shades. Two-pack fillers are perhaps the strongest, so are particularly suitable for deep filling.

Plaster of Paris
Although it is a traditional filler, plaster of Paris has a tendency to go white with age. However, it remains a useful means of flattening rough surfaces (such as chipboard) before applying special paint effects that hide the grain. Wipe plaster of Paris dry with linseed oil. This makes the filler transparent.

Applying grain filler
▲ **1** *Grain fillers are supplied in tins, by weight, in a range of colours. This one is medium mahogany. They are used to fill the open pores in the grain to produce a "full finish"*

and to save later coats of polish. They often settle in storage, and will need stirring to a thick consistency before use.

▲ **3** *Use hessian to apply the thick grain filler. Take a hand-sized piece of hessian and bunch it into a swab, before dipping it into the grain filler. The swab must be well charged with filler.*

▲ **4** *Rub the swab over the surface using a circular motion, keeping it wet at all times and sliding across the surface, to push the*

filler gently into the pores. Apply more grain filler as required and keep rubbing until the whole surface has been covered.

▲ **2** *Prepare the surface to be filled by sanding, and staining if required. Make sure the surface is clean of dust and dirt so that the grain filler clings effectively to the timber.*

▲ **5** *Wipe off surplus filler with a clean piece of hessian, working across the grain. (For fillers that can be thinned with white spirit, wipe off across the grain with a rag damped with white spirit.)*

▲ **6** *Once filled, the surface loses some of its grain pattern. This surface will have to be very lightly sanded to remove surplus filler.*

Mixing plaster of Paris filler

▶ **1** *Plaster of Paris is a traditional grain filler which can be mixed with pigments. It is good for deep pores but it does tend to turn white with time. Traditionally, the surface was rubbed with linseed oil to "kill" the whiteness. However, plaster of Paris can cause problems if used under AC lacquer.*

◀ **2** *Mix the pigments and plaster of Paris on a piece of thick paper or card. The colour of the mixed plaster and pigments is roughly the same as it will be once dry in the pores of the wood.*

▶ **3** **(inset)** *Dip a clean piece of hessian into a shallow container of water and then mix with the plaster to create a creamy mixture that is ready to apply.*

▲ **4** *Apply with circular motions, and then along the grain. The filler will dry quickly.*

HINTS AND TIPS

- Do not overthin fillers.
- Test filler on a piece of scrap wood.
- Always wipe off filler across the grain.
- Fillers dry light, so always start with a colour darker than the workpiece.
- Fill after staining, and seal with a thin coat of shellac sanding sealer.
- White-spirit-based fillers can be mixed with solvent wood dye.

MEMO

❖

Tools and materials
Hessian or coarse cloth

Grain filler

Soft cloth

White spirit

Abrasive paper

❖

Common problems
Fillers can turn white if not allowed to dry thoroughly.

Clarity of finish can be lost with the use of fillers.

Fillers not wiped off completely can result in a patchy finish.

Wood stain may be partly removed when sanding back surplus filler if the stain is applied before filling.

❖

Appropriate surfaces
Grain fillers are popular for open-grained timbers, such as oak and ash. They can also be used on close-grained timbers such as mahogany and walnut.

❖

Drying time
Plaster of Paris dries in about 15 minutes.

Oil-bound fillers take up to 3 hours to dry.

Allow 1 to 1½ hours for other fillers to dry.

3

Basic finishing techniques

Most woodworkers are introduced to finishing by the varnishing of DIY projects. Varnish can be the perfect finish for specific tasks, but there are times when French polishing, oiling and waxing are more suitable – and they are surprisingly easy to accomplish

French polishing

The simple principle of French polishing is to build up a lustrous finish with thin coats of transparent or coloured polish. The joy of this finish is that it is worked into the surface, rather than laid on top like a paint, varnish or sprayed lacquer.

Few tools are needed, and the small stock of materials can be bought either ready-mixed or in a raw state for home mixing. Start by buying proprietary brands – then, as confidence grows, you can try mixing your own polish to suit the needs of particular jobs. As a general description the term French polishing is now something of a misnomer, as French polish is only one of the many shellac-based products sold by finishing suppliers. However, "French polisher" remains the time-honoured title of the skilled craftsmen who undertake this style of finishing.

French polish in its many guises is perhaps most highly regarded on mahogany, as the close grain of the wood is admirably suited to the finish and its attractive figure is enhanced by the "depth" of the polish. Timbers such as walnut, rosewood, sycamore and stained pine are equally suitable. Oak is less so, and is given a wax finish more often than not.

Practice

The essential components of a polishing kit box (shellac, methylated spirits and linseed oil, with a "polishing rubber" for application) have hardly changed over hundreds of years, though the original formula for French polish died with its Parisian inventors in the eighteenth century.

When applying French polish, the (Continued on page 62.)

Making a rubber
▲ **1** *The polishing rubber is used to apply French polish. Start by folding a 150mm (6in) square piece of wadding in half. (Cotton wool can be used but the result will not be as good.)*

▲ **2** *Fold over the ends of the wadding to make a point. At this stage it will look a little like a pointed hat.*

▶ **3** *Fold the long ends towards the centre and tuck them in.*

◄ **4** *Work the wadding into a pear shape. It is important the sole is flat when held between the fingers. The idea is to produce a firm core to the polishing rubber.*

▲ **7** *Make another fold and turn the ends together under the core, folding the cloth and forming a point.*

MEMO

❖

Tools and materials
Polish to suit

White cotton cloth

Wadding or cotton wool

Linseed oil

Fine silicon-carbide paper

Methylated spirits

Airtight container

▲ **5** *Place the wadding core diagonally on the corner of a piece of 225mm (9in) square white cotton cloth with the sole of the wadding* *facing downwards. The cloth must not be starched or coloured.*

▲ **8** *Pull the excess cloth across and start to twist together to tighten.*

▼ **9** *Make a final twist, bringing all the loose ends together, and leaving nothing hanging.*

❖

Common problems
Uneven pressure while bodying up can create ridges.

Concentrating only on the centre of the piece will create a sheen there – but not in the corners and along the edges.

A cold or humid environment can cause "chilling" in the finish, similar to the white rings produced by hot water or alcohol.

❖

Appropriate surfaces
French polishing can be used on most timbers.

▲ **6** *Turn the cloth over and hold the core between index finger and thumb to let the folds of the cotton cloth* *drop down to the sides. Make a fold to form the point.*

▶ **10** *When not in use, the rubber must be stored in a sealed container.*

❖

Drying time
The first coat of polish dries in an hour. Keep bodying up until the surface is too sticky to continue (because it has started to dry) – then leave overnight before embarking on the next bodying up session. It is also best to leave the results of the second bodying up to dry overnight, as it tends to sink.

59

WHAT IS SHELLAC?

● It is likely to remain a mystery how anyone discovered that the excretion of the female *Lacifo lacea* beetle is an ideal substance for polishing furniture. In fact, shellac has been used for finishing for thousands of years. Traces of it have been found in Egyptian tombs and on artefacts from ancient China and Rome. Nowadays it is an ingredient of hair spray, confectionery, paints and sealers, and it is even employed as a coating for electrical components.

● The history of French polishing is sketchy, but it is known that the process was first practised by the brothers Etienne and Simon Martin in Paris around 1730. They combined shellac with alcohol, in an attempt to emulate the Japan lacquer finish that was popular on imported furniture.

● Today, although alcohol has been replaced by industrial alcohol, shellac is still produced by traditional techniques. It is sold in a variety of forms, ranging from raw flake to bleached polish, and there is even a version resistant to hot water.

● Flake shellac is the most common raw product, and is ready for dissolving in meths. The proportion of shellac to meths is known as the "cut". When 900g (2lb) of shellac is mixed with 4.5l (1gall) of methylated spirits, the polish is referred to as a 2lb cut. This terminology continues today, even though the polish is sold by the litre. Most finishers buy 4lb or 3½lb cut polish and then thin it to their own requirements. Start by using this with some white polish and some garnet polish.

Sealing the surface

▶ **1** *Sealing the surface with an initial coat of shellac is known as fadding up. Use a piece of wadding that has previously been used in a rubber (a new piece will leave fluff on the surface). Charge it with polish from an unbreakable container of polish, with a small hole or slot in the lid to let the finish out slowly. Add about 2 teaspoons of polish into the wadding.*

◀ **2** *Squeeze the wadding to remove any excess polish. The wadding must feel damp, but not soaking wet. Squeeze the polish onto a clean piece of paper, making sure no dirt or dust is picked up by the wadding. The workbench is not a good surface for this operation.*

◀ **3** *Wipe the wadding across the surface following the grain. Use no pressure at all to start with, for two or three passes. Continue to apply the polish in tight circles, and as the wadding dries out increase the pressure, recharging when it dries out completely. Continue to work the surface until it becomes too sticky. Leave to dry.*

Motions for applying polish with a rubber

Straight strokes must follow the grain

Interlocking figure-of-eight for bodying up

Wide figure-of-eight motions

Interlocking circles to produce an even coat

Wide circles for initially spreading the polish

▲ **4** *When the shellac coat has dried, the surface will feel rough. Lightly sand (a process known as denibbing) using fine 320 silicon-carbide self-lubricating abrasive paper. Press down flat. Make sure that all the surface is sanded, working gently across the grain and in circular motions. Always keep the paper flat on the surface.*

French polished oak table
▲ *This round dining table has been French polished to give a subtle, natural looking finish.*

aim is to avoid creating marks – so the polishing rubber is designed to work the mixture of shellac and methylated spirits evenly across the surface, lubricated by linseed oil. Try at all times to use a flowing action, keeping the rubber continually on the move.

To achieve the smoothness of a grand piano (the ultimate aspiration of French polishers, though pianos are now often sprayed), the preparation has to be faultless. If you want a full grain effect, fill the open pores with grain filler (see pages 53-55) and then sand through the grades (see pages 18-22), making sure the grain has been raised and that you sand it flat.

French polish is particularly sensitive to water and alcohol – as any dining table will testify – so check there is no damp on the surface, or you will find that it shows up later. If necessary, heat out any dampness with an iron over sheets of brown paper. When staining the piece, remember that the methylated spirits in the polish is likely to soften spirit stains and affect the colour.

Bodying up

Once a sealing coat has been applied (a process known as fadding up) and the surface has been lightly sanded (denibbed) and dusted, you can start applying the polish to body up the finish. Start with straight strokes following the grain, then across the grain. Maintain a slight pressure. The pressure is like that needed to plaster walls or spread butter on toast. Having covered the surface two or three times, continue with circular movements, which help to smooth out the polish. Try to maintain even pressure throughout each circle; there is a tendency to press harder as your hand moves towards your body on the inward stroke. Use 12-15cm (5-6in)

CHARGING A POLISHING RUBBER

- The polish must soak through the core, but must not then drip through the outer cloth. You need to be able to produce a small trickle by cupping the rubber in your hand (with your forefinger running along the point) and gently squeezing.

- If you do accidentally overcharge the rubber, squeeze out the excess until the steady flow stops, then wipe on a piece of clean scrap to dry off the surface.

- Use a bottle of polish for charging the rubber. For better control of the flow, punch holes or cut a slit in the lid of the bottle.

- Store the rubber in an airtight jar after use (never store in a metal container). You do not want to throw away a polishing rubber, as they take time to break in and a new one is not as easy to use. However, you will have no option but to throw away the rubber if it goes hard.

---

circles, making sure the rubber covers the circle. Larger pieces, such as table tops, need larger polishing rubbers; the opposite is true of smaller items.

Maintain the flow of polish with increased pressure whenever the rubber seems to stick or drag. The surface is likely to soak up polish fast at this stage, so you will have to charge the rubber frequently as the flow dries up. Continue to work the polish in with a combination of circular and figure-of-eight movements, keeping the rubber constantly on the move.

Try to keep the rubber away from soft areas of polish. Test to see if the finish is tacky – and if it is, leave it to harden for a few minutes.

When the finish develops an overall sheen, finish off with straight strokes, following the grain, and leave to dry.

Colour matching

Any discrepancies in the colour will show up once the polish has dried. Wooden pins in chair joints may be too light, and there may be shading around joins in veneer. Stand back and take a good look at the piece to get an

Bodying up

▲ **1** *Once the surface has been sealed and lightly sanded it is time to start applying polish using a polishing rubber; this is known as bodying up. First, charge the rubber with polish by opening up the outer layer of* cloth and pouring polish into the core until it is saturated. Squeeze out the excess by pressing on to paper or a spare piece of wood.

▲ **2** *Body up the polish with straight strokes along the grain, making 4 or 5 passes. Then move the rubber in circles. Increase the pressure as the rubber dries out, and then* charge again. Use figure-of-eight patterns as well as circles.

▶ **3** *After working the surface with 4 or 5 applications it will become sticky, and the rubber will need to be lubricated with linseed oil. Dip your finger in the oil, and rub it onto the sole. Do not use too much oil. Continue working the rubber in circular motions.*

▼ **4** *The bodying up will have built up a finish by now, but continue to work the rubber around the piece, in circles, figure-of-eight movements and straight up and down. Charge the rubber when it dries out, doing so little but often.*

WHICH POLISH IS WHICH?

The technique is called French polishing but the polishes used have different names and different applications.

French polish
French polish is brown (it is also known as brown polish), and is used mainly on mahogany.

Button polish
A golden brown colour.

Garnet polish
This is dark brown, and is recommended for renovation of old surfaces.

White polish
White polish is made from Shellac that has been bleached and is milky white. It is used for light timbers, such as sycamore and ash.

Transparent polish
Transparent polish is made from shellac that has been bleached and dewaxed.

HINTS AND TIPS

- Always keep the rubber well charged – but never with too much polish.
- Use linseed oil sparingly – little and often is best.
- Try to maintain an even pressure when using the rubber.
- Work in a dust-free environment.

- To clear excess polish from a rubber, simply press it down onto a clean surface.
- Keep your fingernails short – as they can scratch the surface and collect dirt, which then falls on the piece during polishing.
- Try to keep the workshop at about 18°C (65°F) for polishing.

overview of the finish. Colour irregularities will need to be touched up and disguised. Look carefully at the surface to judge which colours are visible, or lacking, in the timber.

Use spirit stains for matching colours, and mix them in with the polish. Go easy with these stains, as the colours are strong and are only required in a much diluted form to produce a tint (see pages 44-49 and 66-69). Remember it is easier to make a surface darker than lighter, so mix colours gradually. Apply the colour with a fad (wadding) or colouring mop. Mix the colour on a piece of paper.

Defects such as knots, glue marks and stopping must be touched up and hidden, using pigments (see pages 66-69). Take care that the pigment does not show up as a blob of solid colour, and if necessary use a pencil brush to add flecks of colour to imitate the grain.

Stopping

Bruises and dents can be dealt with at this stage. Fill the indentations with wax stopper, using a small knife to press the wax in. Once it is dry, smooth off with the back of a piece of abrasive paper. You may need to touch up these defects, using a coloured cellulose wax.

Finishing off

You are now ready to finish off the surface, using the rubber, which should be ready for use in its airtight container. Charge with polish, and start working on the surface. If the rubber starts to drag, put a touch of boiled linseed oil on the sole for lubrication. This will leave a smear on the surface. As an even coat of polish appears, start working the rubber "dry", charging only with meths, to

Matching colours for touching up
◀ **1** *The scratch on this piece has removed the colour and revealed the raw timber. The damage can be touched up, using spirit colours.*

◀ **2** *Mix the spirit colours together by adding a small amount of stain to a 50:50 solution of polish and methylated spirits. Use a No. 6 pencil brush. Compare the colour against the workpiece by dabbing it onto a scrap of wood or a piece of card.*

◀ **3** *Use the tip of the brush only to touch up the scratch, and keep your hand as steady as possible. Build up the repair gradually, with a small amount of colour at a time until it matches the surrounding area. Try to imitate the grain pattern as you brush.*

◀ **4** *Do not touch up in one application, but build up gradually. Once the scratch has been repaired it must be polished to match the rest of the surface.*

level the surface.

Finally, charge the rubber with polish and, using straight strokes, work along the grain from end to end; this is known as stiffing off. Leave to dry once a gloss finish has been achieved.

Spiriting off

For a really high-gloss finish, charge the rubber with methylated spirits only and work over the surface with circular and straight movements. The polishing rubber must feel cold to the touch, and not moist. Spiriting off will take off the last of the remaining oil and give the surface a high-gloss finish.

Dulling

A satin or matt finish is popular, as it provides a more natural-looking finish. Instead of polishing with a meths-charged rubber, dull the piece, when dry, with pumice powder or fine wire wool and wax. The pumice powder can be applied straight onto the surface and worked with a dulling brush. Follow the grain, using a mop for dulling mouldings and corners.

When dulling with wire wool and wax (see pages 73-75), do not use too much wax. Once the surface is dry, wipe off the excess with a clean soft cloth to produce a satin finish. The wire wool needs to be fine – either 000 or 0000 grade. However, test the wire wool on a practice piece before dulling, to find out which grade is suitable. Sometimes 0000 wire wool is so fine that it actually glosses the surface.

Before and after dulling
▲ *Dulling with pumice powder reduces a high gloss to a more natural satin finish. This finish is useful for restoration, and can be lightly waxed. There are many grades of pumice. It is essential that a very fine grade is used. 300 mesh would be satisfactory.*

Dulling with pumice powder
▲ **1** *Pour the pumice powder into a shallow tray. Pour carefully, making sure the powder does not spill around the work.*

▲ **2** *Use a dulling brush to apply the powder. This is a specialized short-hair brush. Dip the brush into the powder, taking up only a small amount at a time. Do not use too much – it makes no difference to the finish and will only have to be cleared up to avoid contaminating other finishes.*

▶ **3** *Work the pumice powder against the piece by following the grain, making sure that all areas are covered and treated evenly. Pumice powder should be kept clean, and stored in a dry place.*

Working with colours

Wood can be coloured with either pigments or dyes. The difference between the two is that dyes are dissolved in a solvent and penetrate into the grain of the wood, whereas pigments are used in suspension and lie on top of the grain. This is why pigments fall to the bottom of a tin, having been mixed with a liquid. They are used for blinding or hiding a defect or knot, or for touching up a polished surface. Dyes are the colouring agents of stains and can be dissolved in spirits (in the case of aniline dyes) or other solvents, such as water or oil.

Dyes and stains

Dyes become part of the timber and are used for matching woods. Their translucence allows the grain to show through. The idea is to use colours to bring out the colour inherent in the timber. This might mean adding warmth with a red dye, or even cutting back red hues by using green. The whole piece may need colouring, or just small parts, especially during restoration or when components do not match within a new piece. It is quite common for the legs or rails of a table to have been milled from a different batch of timber from that of the top. As a result the colours may vary slightly, but this can be rectified using dyes.

Study the wood to determine what colours are needed to match it exactly. The best way to learn is by trial and error, so always test colour on a variety of surfaces to see what effect it has. With practice you will understand better the consequences of colour, and should be able to judge the match by testing colours on scraps of timber.

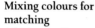

Mixing colours for matching
▲ 1 To camouflage new or restored sections of a piece with matched colours, mix spirit stains with polish and methylated spirits to produce a translucent colour that does not mask the grain. A traditional paper "boat" is being used to mix the colours but any non-food container can be used.

▲ 2 Mix the shade required by adding a small quantity of colour at a time. Use a No. 6 pencil brush to mix the colours with a 50:50 combination of methylated spirits and polish. Make sure the colour is thoroughly blended into the polish and methylated spirits.

Do not try to obtain a perfect match in one go, but gradually blend the colour in with a progression of dyes. Try to copy the subtle differences in colour and shade of the grain pattern, and apply the colour with brushes or mops for small areas, and wadding for larger ones. Look for distinctive colour or what is known as "natural flash". This refers to the fact that the colour is seen from varying angles because of the honeycomb structure of the timber. Wenge has little natural flash, and has a flat constant colour. If possible, colour a piece with it standing at the appropriate level. For example, stand a chair on the floor and place a clock at chest height.

Most timbers are shades of brown, ranging from the beige of light oak to the black colour of ebony, with countless shades in between. Many woods can be matched using Bismarck brown (which is a reddish colour) and spirit black, with green, blue and yellow for adjustment. Remember that black and red make brown. Look for the colours in the timber.

Colour matching
▶ 1 *The frame of this mirror unit is slightly lighter in colour than the rest of the unit. It needs to be colour matched before the piece can be finished.*

▲ 2 *Mask the mirror glass with paper, stuck down with a few small tabs of double-sided sticky tape. Use wadding to apply the colour. Dip the wadding into the boat of colour, only taking up a little of the liquid. Do not try to use too much colour at a time.*

▲ 3 *Squeeze out excess colour from the wadding on a piece of paper or card. Do not do this on the top of the workbench, where the wadding is likely to pick up dirt and dust. Squeezing out the wadding on paper also spreads the colour through the wadding, which makes an even application easier. Remember that only a shade of colour is being applied.*

▶ **4** *Wipe the colour onto the surface using straight strokes. Follow the grain and keep an even pressure. Do not start applying a second stroke of colour until the first has dried. Applying more colour to wet colour is likely to produce a patchy finish. Build up the colour gradually until the required shade is achieved.*

▶ **5** *When the colour work is done, the frame should match the rest of the piece. The colour must be constant. This technique can also be used for matching new veneer that has been let in as a repair.*

HINTS AND TIPS

• Colour piece with it standing at the appropriate height, for example stand a chair on the floor and place a clock at chest height.

• Mix pigments on a piece of paper for quick colouring.

• Use dyes to obtain the right colour match.

• Use pigments to blind out defects.

• Mix colours gradually.

• Work in natural light.

• Study colour of timber and grain pattern.

Pigments

Pigments have to be mixed together before being applied, in order to produce the correct colour. Unlike dyes, they are not translucent, so one layer has little influence upon the next They have colourful names, but a finisher only really needs about eight different pigments, which can be mixed with methylated spirits and/or French polish to create the desired result. When using pigments in conjunction with polish, add the coloured polish to the polishing rubber, or use a colouring mop. Pigments are strong and only need to be mixed in very small quantities, using a filling knife to pick up the powder.

Use a pencil brush to apply pigments on defects. It is important to keep a steady hand. Signwriters use a stick with a pad to rest the hand on, but an extended finger against the surface will often do.

MIXING COLOURS

- Yellow ochre and white make light oak.

- Yellow ochre, titanium white and Bismarck brown make mahogany.

- Brown umber and black make dark oak.

- Brown umber and yellow ochre make brown oak.

- Brown umber, white and yellow ochre make walnut.

- Orange chrome and yellow chrome colour out black marks.

Oil colours

◀ *Howard Raybould has used contrasting oil colours on this column. He applies artists' oils with a brush and then rubs the colour into the grain with a soft cloth or his fingers.*

Using masks

▲ *Howard Raybould coloured the top and legs of this occasional table with oils, and sprayed the side pieces, masking out specific areas with odd pieces of plywood.*

Oil finishes

Oiling is one of the oldest treatments for preserving and finishing wood. Originally linseed oil was used, which is derived from flax and dries by oxidation. Today, oil finishes are becoming increasingly popular, as they can be restored and maintained easily – and, unlike varnishes and sprayed finishes, do not conceal the timber's tactile qualities.

It is true that oils do not have the resistance of more modern finishes, and oiled surfaces are likely to become marked. However, they are not as vulnerable as French-polished surfaces.

Teak and Danish oils dry faster than linseed, and they represent the easiest method of finishing wood.

If you want to stain the wood, do so before oiling. Use a water stain (see pages 44-49) – avoid solvent wood dyes, as they react with the finish, resulting in patchy colouring.

Linseed oil

A linseed-oil finish is simple to produce. However, it takes time to dry and new wood will need a number of coats, especially if it is porous. During

Oiling

▼ **1** *Oil finishes can be used on most timbers, to bring out the natural qualities of the wood. Apply the oil – be it linseed, tung or Danish – with a soft cloth. Charge the cloth with enough oil to apply a wet, even coat to the surface.*

▲ **2** *Rub the oil evenly into the whole surface. It is important to check that the grain is completely wetted, otherwise the finish will turn out patchy. Use circular strokes at first,* then straighten up and follow the grain to finish.

▲ **3** *Leave the oil to dry overnight. Some deep grained timbers will have soaked up most of the oil, leaving little on the surface. Lightly sand the rough surface with fine 320 self-lubricating abrasive paper. Apply* further coats until the required finish is achieved, leaving each coat overnight to dry and lightly sanding between applications. Three or four coats of oil is usually enough.

◄ **4** *Drying time varies between hours and days, depending on the type of oil (see "Memo" box, right). When dry, take a palm-sized piece of fine 0000 wire wool to give the surface a final sheen. Rub in the direction of the grain, keeping an even pressure and stroke over the whole piece to produce a satin finish.*

▶ **5** *Burnish the surface with a clean soft cloth to remove any dust that might have been left after rubbing with wire wool.*

◄ **6** *Oils heat up as they dry – by oxidation – and this can be a fire hazard if they are left screwed up on the bench or in a bin. Dispose of used rags by dousing them in a bucket of water. If left overnight the rag will be safe to throw away.*

MEMO

Safety precautions
Never leave an oily rag rolled up. As the oil oxidizes, it generates heat and can combust spontaneously.

Allow oily rags to dry outdoors, unrolled, if you need to keep them for further use. Do the same before you throw them away.

Tools and materials
Flat brush

Soft, lint-free cloth

Silicon-carbide abrasive paper

0000 wire wool or a plastic scouring pad

Common problems
When finishing thin pieces, there is a chance that they will warp as the oil dries.

Appropriate surfaces
Any timber can be oiled. Teaks, rosewood, afrormosia and oak are often treated with an oil finish.

Drying time
Raw linseed oil takes 3 days to dry.

Boiled linseed oil takes 24 hours to dry.

Teak and Danish oils take 12 hours to dry.

Leave polyurethane oil overnight to dry.

71

HINTS AND TIPS

• To thin linseed oil, so it is easier to apply, pour the oil into a container and stand it in a pot of very hot water.

• Enough oil has been applied when patches appear.

• Oil will darken the surface of the wood.

• Non-toxic or edible oils, such as olive oil, must be used for salad bowls and other items that come into contact with food.

the complex process of oxidation raw linseed oil actually gains weight as it dries, but it does not dry as fast as the boiled variety. Boiled linseed is partially oxidized and takes a day to dry – compared with three days for pure linseed, which is more resistant to external conditions. However, neither linseed oil nor boiled linseed oil are suitable for oiling exterior woodwork.

Apply the oil by cloth and rub it into the timber. Leave it to dry for at least 24 hours. You can try mixing linseed oil equally with white spirit for the first few coats, to encourage the finish to penetrate the timber and dry faster. After that, apply the oil neat until a surface film is achieved. Warming linseed oil lowers its viscosity and aids penetration. However, it combusts easily, so the safest way to warm it is to pour the oil into a container and stand it in a pot of very hot water. Check whether the oil has dried, by wiping a hand across the surface and looking for oil marks, before applying the next coat. Once you are satisfied with the finish, buff with a soft cloth.

Teak and Danish oils

Teak and Danish oils dry faster than linseed, and provide a more resistant film on the surface. Teak oil produces a slight sheen; Danish oil leaves a more natural, low lustre. They are better for

Bringing out wood's natural beauty

▶ *The use of an oiled finish on this box has brought out the natural, rich patina of the wood, making it look extremely attractive and providing excellent surface protection. All oil finishes are relatively easy to apply, but the process takes time, especially if porous new wood is involved.*

new pieces; use linseed on older ones. Some of these oils are tinted for colour. They all include driers, and sometimes tung oil to enhance their protective nature. You can buy pure tung oil, which comes from the seeds of the Chinese tung tree. It is used in a similar manner to Danish or teak oils.

Apply these oils with a cloth or flat brush. Do not use too much oil at a time, as it will not all sink in. Leave to dry for about 24 hours before applying the next coat, sanding down with fine silicon-carbide paper between applications. Most surfaces will take about three or four coats, but the number of coats is largely a matter of choice and judgement. If the finish is too thin and starts to get dirty, apply more oil.

Oil varnish

An even stronger oiled finish can be achieved by mixing linseed oil with oil varnish. This produces a thicker coating than oil on its own and also burnishes better.

Oil varnish is available ready-mixed, but one recipe is to mix about 2 parts white spirit (or turpentine) and oil to 1 part varnish. Experiment with the proportions to arrive at the desired finish. Turpentine and white spirit are generally interchangeable for thinning (natural turpentine, as opposed to turps substitute, has a distinctive pine smell).

Apply with a cloth or flat brush, then leave to dry. For a gloss finish, burnish with a soft cloth once the surface is dry; for a satin or matt sheen, rub with 000 wire wool and wax (see pages 73-75).

Waxed finishes

Waxing is a traditional way of protecting and enhancing timber. Wax finishes have been found on Jacobean furniture, beeswax was used by the ancient Egyptians, and to this day wax remains the most popular finish for oak. Indeed, only the introduction of French polishing diminished the popularity and general use of wax. Waxing produces a natural finish; like an oiled surface, it is never complete and the constant rubbing by hands continues to improve the finish, deepening its patina, over the years.

Beeswax and carnauba wax have been the most consistent ingredients of furniture wax. The two are often mixed together with turpentine, by warming, to produce hard but compliant waxes. Carnauba adds strength and is often an ingredient of floor polishes. Woodturners use carnauba in stick form to produce a friction finish, holding the stick against the turning piece then buffing it with a soft cloth. Care has to be taken not to press the cloth too hard, in case that melts the wax and tears it .

Tinted wax polishes can be used on dark or light woods. The dark waxes are particularly useful for restoration work and for creating antique effects. Some of the darker timbers benefit from treatment with a dark water stain, to deepen their colour further, before waxing.

As with any finish, it is important to prepare the workpiece carefully. Apply two thin coats of shellac sanding sealer before waxing, to protect the timber and fill the pores. Sand with fine silicon carbide (see pages 20-22) between and after the coats of sealer.

Today there are many mixed waxes available in cream, paste or stick form. Some are coloured, with the dark antique variety especially good for working old oak. Waxes work well on a stained surface – but do not use over solvent wood dye (see pages 44-49). It is also possible to mix in pigments to achieve special effects.

Waxing
▶ **1** *Waxing will give this old oak tray more life and bring out the grain.*

73

▲ **2** *Apply the wax with a soft cloth folded into layers. Pick up the wax on the cloth, and rub it liberally into the grain using a circular motion.*

Level off following the grain. Make sure the surface is covered evenly and thoroughly.

USING BEESWAX

Beeswax is sold commercially, refined and ready for use, as cake or block. It also provides the basis for many manufactured wax finishes.

It is, of course, possible to obtain beeswax in a more natural form, as a honeycomb, from a beekeeper. The honey will have been removed, usually by centrifuging. In order to use the wax for finishing, melt the honeycomb in a water heater or glue pot until liquid. Be careful when heating it, as wax is highly flammable. When the waste rises to the top, skim it off and throw it away. Let the wax cool and resolidify, then add 5 per cent linseed oil to keep it soft.

Although the colour is normally yellow, beeswax can be bleached to produce a white wax, which is harder and more brittle. The melting point of beeswax is about 65°C (150°F). If you want to harden it, mix it with carnauba wax, which comes from the Brazilian wax palm and has a melting point of 85°C (185°F). You can also add paraffin wax or candle wax to make the finish easier to apply.

If you buy beeswax in block or cake form, use a cheese grater to grate it into a glass container, then cover with turpentine and leave overnight. This produces a paste that can be applied liberally with a brush and left to dry for 12 hours. It works well for intricate carvings and turned wood. When the first application is dry, apply more paste until a coating is built up and the surface can be burnished with a soft lint-free cloth.

◀ **3** *Leave the piece to dry for 15 minutes and then apply further coats of wax with fine 000 wire wool, rubbing with the grain. Build up the finish gradually, leaving each coat overnight to dry. Four or five coats should be enough.*

▼ **5** *After waxing, the oak tray's real beauty is apparent.*

◀ **4** *For a more lustrous finish, buff the waxed surface with a soft cloth. Do not press too hard – it is possible to break up the even coat of wax.*

**The finished
wax polish**
▲ *The polish is ready for
use when it has cooled
thoroughly.*

**Making wax polish
from beeswax**
▲ 1 *Grate beeswax and
carnauba wax into
flakes onto clean paper,
with 10 parts beeswax to
1 part carnauba.*

◄ 2 *Melt the wax in a tin
or old saucepan over a
gas or electric hob or use
a specialized water
heater, as here. Do not
boil the melted wax
because this can cause
discoloration. Melting
takes about 10 minutes.*

◄ 3 *Remove the
saucepan from the heat,
then pour 10 parts
turpentine to 1 part*
*melted wax into the
heater. Stir as you pour,
until the mixture is
creamy.*

▲ 4 *When the mixture
has reached the right
consistency and all the
flakes are dissolved,
pour it into a shallow
container. Leave to cool
for some time to produce
an even consistency.*

HINTS AND TIPS

• Seal with shellac sanding
sealer before waxing.

• Make sure the wax is dry
before further applications.

• To remove wax, rub down
with white spirit and wire wool.

Wipe off the solution formed
with a clean rag or paper kitchen
towels.

• The final finish depends on
the burnishing, rather than the
build-up of wax.

Varnishing

HINTS AND TIPS

• Decant varnish into a paint kettle and attach a wire across the top of the kettle so you can wipe off excess varnish from the brush.

• Make sure there is no dust in the workshop. Sprinkle the floor with water, and make sure your clothes are free from hairs and dust.

• Use a good-quality brush for varnishing. A cheap paintbrush would produce a very poor varnished finish.

• Press with a thumbnail to test varnish for hardness.

Varnishes come in a variety of forms, with different properties and a range of applications. Unlike polishes, they sit on the surface of the timber as a coat. Some have good waterproofing qualities, others are fast-drying. Today they are known by their resin ingredients, polyurethane being the most common. They are applied by brush, and are available in gloss, matt and satin finishes. The matt and satin varnishes contain a matting agent to produce an irregular surface that doesn't reflect light with the same directness as gloss. A matt finish shows the nature of the timber better than gloss, on which reflections tend to hide the figure.

It is certainly well worthwhile investing in a good-quality varnish brush. They can be expensive but they can make the difference between a good job and a bad one. See what's available at your local DIY shop.

Varnish stains

These varnishes, which are ready-mixed with stain, are supplied in a variety of colours. Some clarity of grain is lost with this type of varnish, but they are useful for covering less attractive timbers. Make sure they are applied evenly, in order to maintain a constant colour.

Polyurethane varnish

Polyurethane has become the symbol for DIY varnishing, since most varnishes in hardware stores are based on this resin. They are available for outdoor use; or with a thixotropic agent to form a gel, which helps on vertical surfaces. Supplied in matt, satin and gloss, they flow well and are

A gloss finish
▲ *See how the rose reflects deeply in the gloss varnish. However, these reflections can sometimes mask the beauty of the wood.*

A satin finish
▲ *The reflection is becoming a blur. The details of the rose are less of a distraction to the view of the grain.*

A matt finish
▲ 1 *A matt varnish produces the most natural finish, bringing out the colour and pattern of the wood and producing little reflection.*

Applying varnish

▼ *Special varnish brushes are made which are worth the extra cost. Apply the varnish across the grain first to spread it evenly over the surface. Then, applying very little pressure,* *draw the brush diagonally across the surface; finish off with the grain exerting a very light pressure. This method will leave the fewest brushmarks.*

▲3 *Leave the waxed piece to dry for an hour or so. Then burnish the waxed surface with a clean, soft cloth. Rub along the grain.*

This will produce a lustrous matt finish, full of colour.

Producing a matt finish

▼ **1** *A better matt finish is obtained by working with gloss varnish than by applying proprietary matt varnishes. First, apply gloss varnish as usual. Then abrade the* *dry surface with fine 000 wire wool. This creates very fine scratches on the surface of the piece, cutting down its ability to reflect light. Always work with the grain, rubbing gently.*

Producing a satin finish

▲ **1** *Use pumice powder and a dulling brush on dry gloss varnish to produce a satin finish. Put a small quantity of pumice powder into a shallow tray.*

▼ **2** *Having rubbed the piece with wire wool, apply wax with a soft cloth following the grain.*

Do not use too much wax, otherwise it will be difficult to buff later.

MEMO

Safety precautions
Varnishes can cause drowsiness, so always work in a well-ventilated workshop.

Wear a mask when sanding.

Take great care when using two-part varnishes, keeping special thinners at hand and ensuring there is a constant draught.

Tools and materials
Paint kettle

Flat brush

Stain, if required

Fine silicon-carbide abrasive paper

White spirit

Linseed oil and pumice powder, or 000 wire wool and wax

Common problems
Applying varnish before the previous coat has hardened, or even when it is starting to go tacky, is likely to mark the finish.

Do not stir thixotropic varnishes – stirring breaks the gel formation.

Drying time
Varnish takes about 6 or 7 hours to dry, but leave overnight between each coat.

Appropriate surfaces
Any timber surface can be varnished.

◄ 2 *A dulling brush has short soft bristles, rather like a shoe brush. Charge the dulling brush with pumice powder by dipping it into the tray and picking up the powder.*

◄ 3 *Once charged, work the dulling brush in straight strokes along the grain over the whole surface. For curved pieces, use a soft cloth, charged with pumice powder. Apply evenly, and do not miss any parts. Keep rubbing until the desired satin finish is produced.*

PREPARING A BRUSH

It is important to prepare a brush for varnishing, otherwise it will shed bristles and also will not soften up. Work the bristles between your fingers, pulling out any loose hairs. Stand the brush in linseed oil, using a wire jig to keep the bristles off the bottom of the container. After a day or so, play the brush backwards and forwards on brown paper; then clean the bristles using white spirit. Straighten the bristles and wrap with clean white paper, fastening with a rubber band around the metal ferrule. Store the brush on its side.

applied by brush – though the final coat must be laid on with as little brushing as possible to avoid streaking.

Water-borne varnishes

Water-soluble varnishes are faster drying and, because of their water base, are non-flammable. Woodworkers intent on finishing their work in an environmentally friendly manner are experimenting with these varnishes. Use a brush for application.

Two-part polyurethane varnishes

These varnishes need an acid catalyst for hardening, and are stronger than standard polyurethane. They are particularly useful for floors and bar tops. They do, however, give off terrible fumes when first applied, by brush, and may react with stains. To achieve a high gloss apply three or four coats and rub down the last coat before burnishing with cream and a cloth. Two coats are sufficient if the lacquer is being rubbed to a satin or matt finish with fine wire wool and wax polish.

Applying varnish

As with other finishes, make sure any defects in the surface have been dealt with, filling holes and cracks and sanding the surface flat. Varnish is more forgiving than other finishes in that it is a coat that can be cut back flat – but it will exaggerate any blemishes through the refraction of light. Clean the piece first with white spirit to remove wax or grease, especially if the surface has been stripped.

Stain the wood, if required. But note that spirit varnishes will pull off spirit stains; and oil-based varnishes will have the same effect on solvent wood dyes. Check the base of the varnish before starting. Make sure any stain is dry before applying varnish, and lightly sand with fine silicon carbide (see pages 20-22) if a water stain has been used.

Manufacturers of varnishes do not recommend thinning, but varnishes based on white spirit are best mixed with about 10 per cent white spirit to aid penetration. Dip the brush in the varnish and work thin coats from the centre of the panel outwards. However, to avoid drips and runs, varnish the edges first. Brush with the grain, then across it, and finally follow the grain, in order to produce an even coat. Try not to brush too hard, as that may leave marks if the varnish is fast-drying, and may also produce bubbles in the finish. If possible, keep the working edge wet all the time, to reduce the chance of an uneven finish.

When the surface is completely dry, cut back with fine paper. Sanding will produce fine white dust; but if the varnish starts to tear up into little balls, it is still too soft and you may need to strip it off and start again. So be careful. Varnish takes time to harden – and though the surface may seem to have set, the same may not be true underneath.

Dust off using a cloth dampened with white spirit, then apply the next coat. Continue until the required depth is achieved, making sure that the last application is even and follows the grain, letting the varnish flow. Most pieces will need two or three coats.

If a satin finish is required when only gloss varnish is available, dull the surface using pumice powder applied with a dulling brush. Charge the brush with powder then work in straight strokes along the grain. To produce a matt finish, use fine wire wool and wax.

Providing a protective finish
▶ *Varnish is a protective finish favoured by joiners and carpenters. It is suitable for fittings that will be exposed to continual wear and tear, such as staircases, windows and doors.*

Restoring old finishes

There comes a time when old furniture and other wooden items need a good clean, without resorting to the drastic action of stripping. Indeed, more often than not there is value in retaining the original finish, since it will have developed a mellow patina that cannot be re-created. A patina that has been built up over the years is one of the most attractive features of antique furniture – but, as with paintings, the surface tends to dull with age and the finish may need to be rekindled by thorough cleaning.

The aim should be to give new life to the finish, not to make the piece look new. The beauty of antique furniture lies partly in its used appearance, in the shades and tones of the timber developed over the years. Cleaning and restoration must therefore be done with great care. It is relatively easy to strip or sand back the wood, but that destroys the finish and detracts from the character of the piece. Always try to conserve, restore and enhance, rather than remove. Remember that the patina is skin deep and does not penetrate far.

Identifying the finish

Before cleaning or embarking on any restoration work, try to identify the finish. This is not always easy. Something about the finish can be deduced from the age of the piece, but previous restorations and renovations may have replaced the original finish with a more modern version.

If the piece was made earlier than the middle of the nineteenth century, then the odds are it was not French-polished originally and is more likely to have been given a finish based on tree resins or fossilized resins. French polishing became common around 1850; later, as furniture production

Cleaning off dirt
▼ **1** *The underframe of this mahogany table needs to be restored. However dirt has built up over the years, and it must be removed before structural repairs or restoration can be started.*

▲ **2** *Use fine 000 wire wool and a proprietary reviver to clean off the dirt. Pour the reviver onto a hand-sized ball of wire wool, using enough to dampen it thoroughly.*

▲ **3** *Rub off the dirt and old wax, following the grain. Make sure to work the wire wool into all grooves and corners. Recharge with reviver regularly. Ensure that the reviver cleans the surface of the piece, but that it does not strip off the finish.*

▼ **4** *The reviving fluid produces a sludge, some of which will get caught up in the wire wool. The rest must be cleaned from the surface with a soft clean cloth. Do this frequently as the sludge can discolour the wood. More than one session of reviving may be necessary to remove stubborn grime.*

moved into the twentieth century, sprayed cellulose finishes were increasingly used.

For a thorough identification, test a small area on a hidden part of the piece, such as the underside of a table or the back of a rail. Apply white spirit with wire wool: this will soften wax, but will not affect French polish or varnish. Always rub carefully and select a spot that will not be easily seen; do not soften the finish too much, or damage may be caused. If white spirit has no effect upon the surface, then the piece has been varnished or sprayed and will have to be stripped with chemicals or sanded back.

Cleaning an old finish

The aim is to clean off dirt and grime that has accumulated over the years. Grease and vestiges of food build up on table tops, while oil from hands has to be removed from the arms of chairs. What is required for cleaning is a formula that will pick up the dirt but leave the patina.

Much grime can be removed with soap and water. Gently wash the surface, but do not overwet it, otherwise the timber may move and joints come apart. For more stubborn areas, use a proprietary reviver or white spirit applied with fine wire wool (000 or even 0000 grade). However, do not use this technique if there are any cracks, as the oil may spread under the finish and lift it off or make the surface murky later.

During the cleaning a sludge will form. Wipe this off with a cloth or with paper towelling. This sludge must be removed before it dries.

Renewing the finish

After cleaning, where appropriate a French-polish finish can be rubbed onto the surface with a polishing rubber – having first filled any small dents with coloured or clear beeswax, touching in with pigments or dyes and a pencil brush (see pages 26–27). Oiled finishes can be restored using linseed oil (see pages 70–72).

If the finish has deteriorated so far

that it cannot be cleaned effectively, it will have to be removed. Use a paint and varnish remover containing methylene chloride (see pages 36–39). Do this with great care – and do not attempt to sand the timber, as sanding would break through the fibres and reveal a new surface. Once the finish has been removed, the surface is ready for oiling, waxing or French polishing, as appropriate. When polishing old furniture, dull the polish to produce an aged look (see pages 73–75).

▲ **5** *Once the piece is dry, apply polish with a fad (wadding). There is no reason to body up a finish – just wipe over to bring back the sheen.*

▶ **6** *The mahogany table is now clean. Note how the colour is stronger and the lines more exact.*

Restoring an armchair

▶ *The most obvious areas of this armchair that need attention are the screw holes on the back and peg holes at the corners on the rails. These should be stopped with wax. The arms must be polished to clean off the dark oil from hands. Check the legs – especially the intricate turning – for marks and dirt.*

Restoring a Davenport

▼ *Ink stains found on the lid of this Davenport (used as a desk) have been removed with bleach or oxalic acid during restoration. Loose veneers on the pen tray have been repaired and stuck down, and old wax and dirt have been cleaned off the legs.*

Restoring an inlaid piece

▲ *Inlay, as on the top of this occasional table, often needs minor repairs. Remove loose pieces of veneer, replacing if necessary and then colour matching. Chips on the edge of the piece can be filled with wax stopper. The table may have been used as a plant stand, so check for water marks.*

4

Decorative finishes

Decorating timber – especially board materials such as MDF (medium-density fibreboard) – with special effects is a craft that has developed with the demands of the market. Fashion and ideas from interior designers have influenced the use of these finishes, and craftspeople have evolved their own techniques and designs. As a result, a wide range of processes and effects are available for the finisher to emulate or use as a medium for innovation

Stippling

Stippling (sometimes referred to as sponging) is probably the simplest of paint effects to produce on timber, fibreboard and walls. By far the best substrate for stippling is MDF, which is smooth and takes finishes perfectly.

Unlike MDF, timber and chipboard need filling with plaster of Paris before stippling (see pages 53-55). Mix the plaster to a paste with water and apply it with hessian, rubbing well into the pores of substrate. Leave to dry and sand flat, using abrasive on a block. The surface is then ready to take the background colour.

The background colour is a matter of choice, so experiment with pastel and darker colours. To mix the colour, blend artists' oil paints with household undercoat or eggshell. Apply the background colour with a flat brush. Leave it to dry, then sand with fine abrasive paper.

For the stipple itself, use emulsion paint, which is easiest to apply. Pour it into a shallow container and mix with other emulsion colours, bearing in mind the shade of the undercoat. Matching colours, only distinguished by a slight difference in shade, may be most suitable – but startling results can be achieved with a contrast.

Applying stipple

Various materials can be used for applying the stipple finish. Each produces its own distinctive effect. Upholstery foam, sponges and paper towelling work well; and there are special brushes, available from decorating suppliers, that are designed to produce individual patterns.

Applying the stipple will need some practice; try it first on a scrap piece of board. Cut up the stippling material into pieces that fit comfortably in your hand. Dip into the colour and squeeze out the excess, so that the pad is damp rather than dripping wet. Dab it over the surface, producing a speckled pattern, replenishing the pad with paint as it dries out. An even pattern is probably the most desirable, but there is no reason why the pattern should not be irregular. If you wish, use more colours and change to different pads.

Alternatively, you can use scumbles or glaze instead of emulsion paint. Scumbles are sold off the shelf, ready-mixed with colour, or you can make your own; glaze can be mixed with artists' oil colours, gold size, white spirit and dryers. Mix the colours to suit and apply with a pad. Both glaze and scumbles take longer to dry than emulsion paint.

Whichever method you choose, once you are certain that the paint is dry, seal the surface with a coat of matt or gloss varnish applied with a flat brush. Polyurethane or oil varnish will alter the colour of the paint.

HINTS AND TIPS

● Practise on scrap board and test effects before stippling.

● Do not apply the stipple too wet.

● Dab the stipple on gently. Do not use too much pressure.

● Make sure scumble or glaze is completely dry before varnishing.

● Vary the way you dab the stipple for a random effect.

● Try different materials for stippling – almost anything will do.

Making a scumble for stippling

▶ **1** *Scumbles can be bought ready-mixed or you can mix your own. To make it, you need artists' colour (sold in a tube), gold size, turpentine or white spirit and linseed oil. You will also need a spatula and a container.*

Select the colour you want to use and place a

small quantity in the container. There is, of course, no reason why more than one colour cannot be mixed together. A rough guide to the proportions required is: 1 part colour to 1 part turpentine, 2 parts linseed oil and 2 parts gold size.

▲ **2** *Thin the colour with turpentine or white spirit. Do not use too much, and stir it all the time.*

▲ **4** *Add gold size to act as a binder and drying agent.*

▲ **3** *Mix in the linseed oil to make the scumble glaze "flow out" when you come to use it. At this stage the mixture must not be too thin, but*

remember that it has to be manipulated with the stipple brush, and so must not be too thick.

▶ **5** *With time, you will develop your own recipe for scumble glaze.*

Creating a stipple finish

▶ **1** *Prepare the surface – in this case MDF – with undercoat, applying it evenly. Start by using a lighter undercoat than the scumble for stippling, but on future pieces experiment with a dark groundwork.*

▶ **2** *Once the undercoat is dry, apply the glaze or scumble thinly, using a flat brush. Lay it on the surface, keeping it wet, and do not brush it around. Do not allow to dry.*

◀ **3** *Hold the stipple brush firmly, and dab over the surface. Maintain an even action as you move around the surface, ensuring that the pressure of each dab is similar. Try not to go over one area more often than others. Keep going until the whole surface has been stippled.*

A selection of different stipple finishes
▲ *Experiment with combinations of colour to produce a range of stippled finishes. Try both contrasting and complementary colours.*
1 *Black background and gold stipple.*

2 *Cream background and orange and yellow stipple.*
3 *Cream background and raw sienna and black stipple.*
4 *White background and green stipple.*

▶ **4** *If desired, use a clean cloth to wipe off a narrow border before the stipple has dried. This gives a more professional finish. Once the glaze has dried, protect it with gloss or matt varnish.*

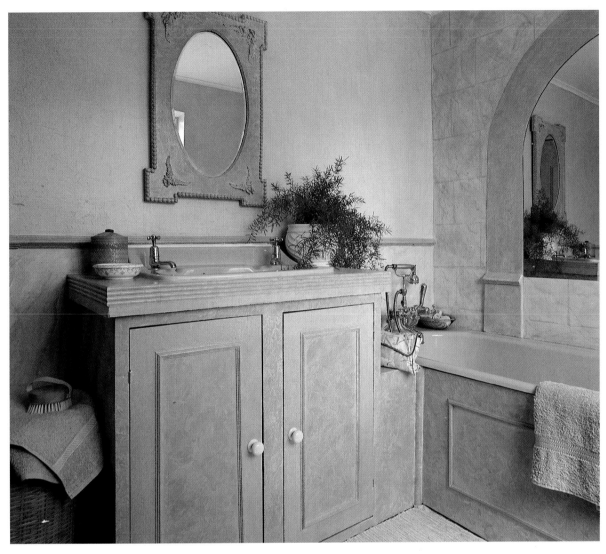

Adding interest
▲ *The wall above the basin unit has been stippled with a grey glaze. Note how the surface is more varied and interesting than a painted grey wall.*

Creating contrasts
▶ *The stippled grey walls above the dado rail contrast well with the heavier effect on the door and woodwork. Below the dado rail, the stipple has been augmented with veins, applied using an artists' brush.*

Graining

HINTS AND TIPS

● Remember when testing scumble colours that the idea is to move wet coats around, combining the various colours, in order to produce the grain pattern.

● Test on scrap materials.

● Look after specialist brushes, as they are expensive.

● Most standard scumbles will need tinting with pigments.

● Make sure each stage has dried before attempting the next application.

Before attempting to reproduce the grain of any timber, take a good look at the natural wood – compare it with other woods, to identify its distinguishing characteristics, and try to memorize its grain pattern and colour. You will notice, for example, that the medullary rays of oak are unique (their appearance depends on the way the timber has been milled); and that mahogany has a distinctive range of red, brown and pink shades. When graining, it may also help to have a piece of the relevant timber available to act as a guide.

Graining is done with scumbles. You can buy these in a range of wood colours, ready-mixed with pigments, gold size, white spirit and dryers. Alternatively, you may prefer to mix your own (see pages 86–87). Scumbles are similar to glaze but dry more slowly, which allows time for graining. They are also of higher viscosity, so thinning may be necessary.

Simple graining tools, which have grooves to simulate grain, are available from DIY stores. Apply the scumble with a flat brush – then, while it is still wet, draw the graining tool across the surface to reproduce the lines of the grain. Bear in mind that grain does not always run straight, but has waves.

Oak graining

Having smoothed the surface and sealed the wood with shellac sanding sealer, use a flat brush to lay down the background colour. For oak, the undercoat should be beige. Leave the

Creating a simple open-grain finish
▼ 1 *Having smoothed the surface and sealed the wood with shellac sanding sealer, apply the* *coloured scumble using a flat brush, laying the finish on evenly over an undercoat. Use long straight strokes, the full length of the piece.*

▶ **2** *Use a comb to etch an open grain pattern into the coloured scumble. Draw the comb across the surface, tipping and rolling it from end to end. Remember that the grain does not always run straight, and has shakes and knots. By rocking the comb from side to side wider patterns are produced.*

▶ **3** *This open-grained effect is designed to imitate pine and other softwoods. Notice how the grain pattern widens and narrows, and contours are produced. Increase the depth of graining with other colours. Once dry, protect the surface with varnish, or stain it.*

MEMO

❖

Tools and materials
Flat brush

Flogger

Badger brush

Pencil brush

Combs

Graining tools

Scumbles

Gold size

Linseed oil

White spirit

Cotton cloth

Undercoat

Varnish

Appropriate surfaces
The ideal surface for a grained finish is MDF, which has no obvious grain and needs minimum preparation.

undercoat to dry, then sand it lightly with fine abrasive paper.

Next, lay down some oak-coloured scumble with a flat brush, using a badger brush to take out the brush marks. Draw a steel graining comb across the surface, making lines in the scumble. Continue right across the surface, making sure each stroke is in line with the preceding one. Wipe the comb clean after each stroke.

Take the comb and draw it across the lines at about 30 degrees. Use a softener or badger to blend the lines in so they match the natural look of timber. Add further figuring with a pencil brush. Make the dark strokes with a pencil brush, softening afterwards. This produces the straight grain of oak.

To create fake medullary rays, prepare the surface in the same way and draw the steel comb over the oak scumble. Soften the effect; then take a flogger (a long broad-headed stiff-bristled brush) and, using a dabbing action, follow the grain, with the flogger laid on its back. This reproduces the flecked appearance of the grain. Traditionally, medullary rays are simulated with the thumbnail, covered with cloth. Alternatively, use the back of a comb wrapped in a cloth.

Once the finish is satisfactory, leave to dry and then apply matt or gloss varnish.

Mahogany graining

After preparing the surface as above, apply a pink-beige undercoat. Sand when dry, then apply the mahogany

Creating a simple close-grain finish

▲ **1** *Having put down an undercoat, and let it dry, apply the scumble as you would for a simple open-grain effect, with long, straight strokes. Make sure the scumble is applied evenly.*

▶ **2** *Work the scumble with a flogger to create the tight, straight grain. Hold the brush loosely and use a beating action along the panel, lengthwise, to produce flecks in the grain.*

scumble with a flat brush, using a curling action to produce the appearance of mahogany figure. Soften the brush marks, then brush with a darker scumble, softening the two coats together.

For straight-grain mahogany apply the scumble with straight strokes of a flat brush, dabbing the grain with the tip of the brush and blending with a badger.

Highlight the grain pattern by dragging a Vandyke water stain across the surface.

Graining and stencilling
▼ *A combination of graining and stencilling has been used to create the interior decoration in this room.*

Graining real wood
▲ *Real wood, such as on doors, which may be in poor condition can be overpainted and then given a painted grain.*

Glaze graining
▲ *A grey-toned paint glaze was brushed on freely. The cross-grains were then scraped out of the wet glaze with a pencil wrapped in a cloth.*

Marbled effects

SEE ALSO

18-19
POWERED
SANDERS

20-21
ABRASIVES

40-43
HOW TO USE
STOPPERS

53-55
GRAIN FILLERS

66-69
WORKING WITH
COLOURS

The most obvious reason for creating a marbled effect is the desire to imitate real marble, and in grand period houses it is not uncommon to find outstanding examples of marbling that are difficult to distinguish from the real thing. The materials used today, which are available off the shelf, are refinements of those used through the ages, but they are more stable and more consistent. Nevertheless, although one batch varies little from another, it is best not to mix batches – and trial and error is the most reliable way to achieve the desired effect.

Preparing the surface

Prepare the substrate, filling the grain if necessary (see pages 53–55). You may want to continue the marbling around corners for three-dimensional realism, so make sure the edges are cleaned up and that holes are stopped and sanded flat. Apply a matt undercoat paint, either acrylic or oil, usually white or pastel. Emulsions may not be the strongest of paints, but they are good enough for practice. With time, you will probably find that the most vivid colours are produced using artists' oil paints, especially glaze. Leave the undercoat to dry, then sand with fine abrasive paper.

▲ **2** *The undercoat is applied as a background colour. It does not need to be white – any colour can be used, to suit the marbling effect desired. Apply the undercoat with a flat brush. When* *it is dry, sand it flat to ensure the surface is as even as is possible.*

Producing marble effects
▶ **1** *The piece ready for marbling. You will need glaze and undercoat, a sponge to mottle and a pencil brush for the veins, a flat brush and badger brush, and linseed oil and colours.*

▲ **3** *Wipe linseed oil over the surface, using a piece of rag, before applying the glaze. This allows the colour to float on the surface, so that it* *can be manipulated before it dries.*

Working with glaze

The next stage is to apply a glaze, for manipulation while still wet. At this point the coloured glazes are not meant to stick to the undercoat, so wipe the surface with linseed oil.

You can buy glaze either in a coloured or clear form. Clear glaze needs to be mixed with coloured oils or pigments, which are supplied in tubes by art suppliers, ready for use. Mix the colours in a shallow container, always using plenty of white. Mix the glaze in equal proportions with gold size and white spirit. Apply a thin layer to the surface, using a flat brush.

While the glaze is still wet, lightly soften the surface with a badger brush (see pages 14–15), evening out the brush marks and producing a slightly mottled effect. Stipple the darker areas with a sponge, then soften with a badger brush once more. The result must look natural, without sharp lines or brush marks.

Add further glaze layers while the previous coat of glaze is still wet. Use thin layers with subtle colours, gradually merging the layers together. This can be repeated until the required effect has been achieved. Make sure that the edges are treated in the same manner, to make the piece look like solid marble.

The veins and streaks are applied

▲ **4** *Apply the glaze with a flat brush, laying it on using straight strokes along the length of the piece. Make sure the glaze is laid on evenly, leaving as few brush marks as possible.*

▲ **5** *Once the glaze has been applied, stipple the surface with a sponge. Use gentle dabs of the sponge, without taking too much paint from the surface. This softens the effect of the glaze, giving it a mottled look. It also removes any brush marks.*

▶ **6** *Soften the effect produced by the sponge with a badger brush. Lightly brush the stippled glaze, blending it in with the background colour. There must be no brush marks left on the surface once this stage has been completed.*

MEMO

Tools and materials
Badger brush

Pencil brush

Flat brush

Feather

Glaze

Artists' oil paints

Gold size

White spirit

Linseed oil

Sponges and cotton cloth

Common problems
It is easy to make the marble too dark, so use plenty of white and develop the colour slowly.

If the softener is not kept clean, it can smudge the effect.

❖

Appropriate surfaces
Use on MDF, if possible, or other flat grainless materials.

❖

Drying time
The glazes will take about 2 hours to dry.

▶ **7** *Use a pencil brush to work in the veins of the marble. Draw across the surface, manipulating the veins by rolling the brush between thumb and finger. Try to produce a random pattern of veins, imitating the natural feel of marble.*

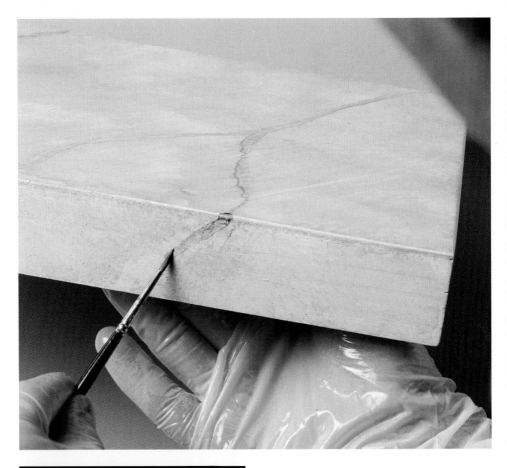

with a pencil brush or a feather. Hold the brush between finger and thumb, and move across the surface oscillating the brush and making irregular strokes. This will form graduated streaks in the glaze, giving a natural effect. Soften these streaks with a badger, blending the glazes.

Another effect to try is splattering. Use a pencil brush charged with glaze, and flick it over the surface. This is best done in concentrated areas. Use the badger for blending. As with any paint effect, there is no end to experimentation with colour and design. Additional glazes can be mixed with dry pigments.

Imitating marble tiles

Real marble is usually stuck in place in panels, like tiles, with thin lines between them. You may want to imitate

A selection of
**different marble
finishes**
▶ **1** *Sky blue
background, red ochre
and black glaze.*
2 *Off-white and pink
background, red oxide
and yellow and red
glaze.*
3 *Off-white
background, raw sienna
and yellow ochre glaze.*
4 *White background,
black and white glaze.*
5 *Black background,
gold glaze.*
6 *Dark green
background, white
scumble glaze.*

▲ **8** *Soften the veins –
again with the badger
brush – to blend into the
overall marble effect.
Brush the surface lightly,
moving the colour in the
veins into the
background colour. Do
not wear away the lines
too far as they will
become indistinct.*

this pattern, in which case paint dark
lines in a grid formation. Marble tiles
vary in size, but are often about 300–
375mm (12–15in) square. Using a
straightedge, draw on the grid before
marbling the area. The tiles need not
necessarily all be the same, and an
interesting effect can be achieved by
altering the colour and grain of the
marble.

▲ **9** *Varnish the finished
piece to protect it from
wear and tear. When
experimenting with
creating a marble effect,
use pale colours at first,
and try blending them
together, as if building
up layers. Look closely
at real marble to see
what you are attempting
to copy. When you
understand how to
manipulate the glaze,
move on to more
dramatic marble effects,
using stronger colours.*

Rag rolling

A traditional way of creating a mottled paint effect on furniture, panelling and walls is to roll the surface with rags before the finish dries. There are any number of techniques used to achieve this decorative effect, from literally rolling cloth across the surface to dabbing the substrate with a rag or other closely knitted cloth.

From a furniture-maker's point of view, MDF is the best substrate on which to work. Other materials need filling with plaster of Paris (see pages 53-55) mixed to a stiff paste, applied with hessian and left to dry before sanding flat (see pages 18-21).

Apply an undercoat and sand back flat. Acrylic paint dries well, but oil-based paints give stronger adhesion. White or pastel eggshell is probably the best base over the undercoat, and can be mixed with artists' oil colours.

When choosing the material for rag rolling, select paints that are compatible with those applied as a base – for example, oil on oil or water on water. Alternatively, mix up paints with glaze and oil colours. The glaze flows more easily, as it contains linseed – but, because of the oil content, take care when drying rags, which can heat up and combust.

Creating a rag-rolled finish

▲ **1** Check the surface of the piece for faults. When any faults have been dealt with, apply the background colour.

An oil-based paint, such as eggshell, gives the best surface for rag rolling, but others can be used.

▲**2** Coat the surface with coloured glaze, using a flat brush and laying the glaze onto the piece, rather than brushing it around. Cover the surface evenly. You are going to move the material around, so do not work so slowly that it dries.

▼ **3** Any material can be used for rag rolling, including cotton cloth, polyethylene or, as in this case, paper towel. Make sure the "rag" is clean before use.

◀ **4** *Roll the paper or cloth into a long roll. It is important that it is not rolled too tightly, and that the surface remains uneven. Different effects can be produced by changing the tightness of the roll, and it is worth experimenting.*

Applying the glaze

Apply the wet coat to the surface thinly. It is important to work fast while the paint is still wet, otherwise it will be difficult to manipulate. The key is to work small areas at a time, having tested the colour on a piece of scrap. Use a soft flat brush, maintaining an even coat.

Do the rag rolling with a piece of cotton cloth rolled around some dowelling. Alternatively, you can simply roll up the cloth, making sure the outside is uneven in order to produce the mottled effect. Keep the effect even across the surface, and always maintain a wet edge as you work.

Rag-rolled panelling
◀ *The panelling behind and around the bath has been rag-rolled. Notice how the effect has been extended up onto the walls. The straight lines are achieved by removing any excess finish using a piece of cloth dampened with white spirit, following a light pencil line.*

MEMO

Safety precautions
Never leave rags containing linseed oil rolled up, as they can spontaneously combust.

Tools and materials
Flat brush

Badger brush

Cotton cloth

Undercoat and eggshell

Plaster of Paris

Coloured glaze

Matt or gloss varnish

Common problems
It is easy to let the colour and effect vary over large areas. Try to keep it even and constant throughout – especially when, after working round a large piece, the first edge meets up with the last.

Appropriate surfaces
You can use rag rolling on furniture, panelling or walls.

Drying time
Leave the eggshell overnight before rag rolling.

Leave the glaze a day or two, to dry thoroughly, before varnishing.

Once the paint is dry, further applications can be made for contrasting colour. Apply a further layer of colour and continue the rolling process. One way of varying the finish is to soften the mottled effect, before it dries, with a softening brush or badger. This is a long-haired brush made from badger hair. Use it to brush the surface lightly with short strokes, just touching the surface. Once it is dry, apply a coat of matt or gloss varnish. Polyurethane or oil varnish will alter the colour of the paint.

Alternative techniques along the same lines include ragging on and ragging off. The first involves applying the coloured glaze directly to the surface, using a fad of rag. Ragging off is identical except that the glaze is applied thin and wet to the surface by brush then mottled by dabbing with the rag. They are both similar to stippling (see pages 86-89).

Which technique is chosen is a matter of ease and convenience, though you are bound to find visual distinctions between the methods.

◄ 5 *Hold the "rag" in both hands and roll it across the wet surface, to produce a mottled effect. Use a badger brush to soften the effect, and leave to dry before applying further glazes.*

▼ 6 *While the final glaze is still damp, if required, wipe off a border around the rag rolled area, using a clean cloth dampened with white spirit. When the glaze has dried thoroughly, apply a coat of gloss or matt varnish to protect it. Bear in mind that polyurethane or oil varnish will alter the colour of the paint.*

HINTS AND TIPS

- Try out colour on scrap before rag rolling.
- Apply thin coats.
- Use new cotton cloth.
- Only attempt small areas at a time.
- Do not let the cloth get too wet.
- Always clean your softener or badger before and after use.

Rag-rolled furniture
◀ *A table and chair in figured birch and fiddle back sycamore, with a rag-rolled panel on the table top.*

Subtle shades
▼ *The colours used on these rag-rolled walls are very subtle, giving a soft feel to the room.*

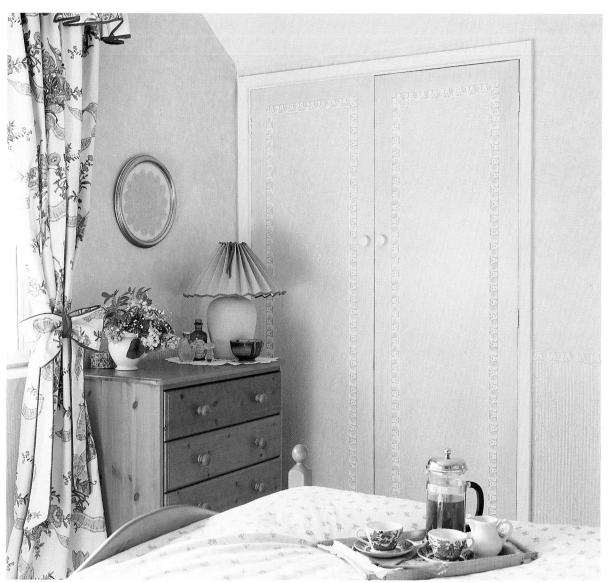

Ebonizing

The rarity and expense of ebony as a natural timber has made ebonizing a popular imitative finish, especially on reproduction Regency furniture and as a substitute for black Chinese lacquer. Today, ebonizing has become synonymous with a uniform finish, with no graining, except for the pores, showing through. Nevertheless, any colour can be used, and often the aim is to create a very dark grey finish with lighter streaks. On mass-produced furniture, a black ash finish is commonly used – usually sprayed on for an even texture, though using black polish instead of spray adds depth to the finish. To simulate the grain structure of ebony and produce a smooth surface, use close-grained timbers such as beech, sycamore or mahogany. There is no reason why the grain should not show through the ebonized finish, though that may make colour matching more difficult.

With ebonizing the slightest imperfection is magnified, so prepare the surface assiduously (fingers are often the best judge of preparation) and take extra care throughout the finishing process.

**Ebonizing a
small chest**
▶ **1** *Ebony is a very dense timber, with very little grain. It is therefore essential that any piece to be ebonized is prepared thoroughly with all the holes and pores filled in and sanded flat. The slightest blemish will be shown up, and exaggerated by the finish. Any idea that black masks faults is unfounded, indeed it shows up mistakes more than any other colour.*

Application

Traditionally, a nigrosine water stain is used for staining the timber. Nigrosine water stain is available by mail order from specialist retailers (see the back of this book for some useful addresses). It's best to avoid using spirit stains for this purpose, especially on a large area; because they dry so quickly, they are difficult to apply. If

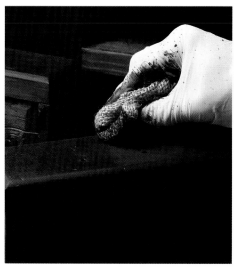

▲4 *Once dry, lightly sand the surface to remove any specks of dust. Then apply black grain filler to fill any open pores. Wipe the filler across the surface with a piece of hessian.*

Clean off any surplus grain filler and leave to dry.

▲2 *Stain the prepared piece with a nigrosine water stain, or a black spirit stain, which is being used here. Apply the stain wet and rub*

well into the grain until an even effect is achieved.

▲3 *You will need to apply plenty of stain to ensure the finish is not patchy. Keep a wet edge at all times, and then wipe off any excess stain with a clean piece of soft cloth.*

Wipe the surface completely clean and then leave the piece to dry.

▲5 *Once the filler has dried, lightly sand and wipe clean. It is now time to start applying the black polish. Use a black spirit stain dissolved in white shellac polish. Use 10 parts of polish to 1 part of stain.*

Charge the polishing rubber with the black polish, and apply as if French polishing.

using a water stain, damp down the surface first to raise the grain, then allow it to dry and sand it flat.

Once the stain has dried, apply white or transparent polish mixed with black spirit stain, using a polishing rubber as for French polish (see pages 58-65). Make a saturated solution of black stain (spirit black in methylated spirits), using about 140ml (¼pt) of stain to 560ml (1pt) of polish. If you want to add lighter streaks, use a colouring mop to apply spirit stain mixed with methylated spirits.

Build up a body of black polish, then leave to dry hard before flatting down with 320 grit garnet paper or silicon carbide of the same grade. Make sure the surface is sanded flat.

To give depth to the finish, apply a final coat of white or transparent polish, using a touch of linseed oil as lubrication. Once the finish looks full enough, spirit off with meths in the polishing rubber to produce a deep gloss. Leave to dry, then burnish with a soft cloth and pumice powder.

▼ 6 *Body up the surface with polish, using a combination of circular, straight and figure-of-eight strokes. Use a spot of linseed oil as a lubricant if necessary. Make sure that the finish is even, checking for patchy areas. Once the polish has been built up, leave to dry.*

▶ 7 *When the body of black polish is completely dry, cut it back with 320 silicon-carbide self-lubricating abrasive paper. The surface must look matt as well as flat – any unevenness will be apparent later. Wipe off the dust and clean the surface.*

▲ 8 *To produce greater depth to the ebonized surface apply white polish. Charge the polishing rubber with white polish and build up the surface as if*

French polishing, until a full gloss finish has been achieved. Leave to dry. If you want a gloss finish, nothing more needs to be done.

HINTS AND TIPS

- Preparation is the key, as defects will be amplified by the finish.
- Use grain filler on open-grained timber.
- Only use spirit dyes for colouring with polish.

▲ **9** *For a satin finish, rub the piece with fine 000 wire wool and wax polish. Rub with the grain and always apply the same pressure,*

otherwise the finish may look patchy and uneven.

▲ **10** *For a final sheen, rub the polished surface with wax and a soft cloth. Rub with the*

grain, covering the whole piece.

◀ **11** *What was once pine is now ebony. It is at this stage that you realize that any blemishes will show up the piece for what it really is.*

Stencilling

SEE ALSO

66-69
WORKING WITH
COLOURS

86-89
STIPPLING

The beauty of stencilling is that it allows anyone, from a complete novice to the most artistic and experienced finisher, to enhance the simplest of finishes with elaborate and attractive decoration.

In America, settlers decorated their homes with stencilling, and the effect became a measure of status. The patterns, which were usually done on a pale background, were taken from pictures or drawn and cut freehand. Today, patterns for stencilling can be bought ready-made from craft shops, and you can use a photocopier to enlarge or reduce images for tracing.

Cutting a stencil

Almost any material can be used for the stencil, but either clear acetate or oiled board is best. Both of these allow the paint or finish to be wiped off easily.

Acetate is perhaps more difficult to cut, as it has a tendency to split – but, being clear, it can be used for direct tracing.

Make sure there is at least a 50mm (2in) border around the pattern, for support. Large motifs may need a wider border. Also, bear in mind that you may want to use the edges as a reference when you are applying the finish. Position the decoration centrally, and trim the edges later.

Use a scalpel or craft knife for cutting the shapes. It is best to use a sheet of glass as a cutting board (pad the edges with masking tape). This avoids the possibility of the blade being deflected by old cut marks, which can happen on cutting boards made from other materials. Only the point of the knife is used for cutting the stencil. It can be sharpened by grinding the back of the blade to create a new tip.

Making a stencil
1 *Draw out the motifs for the design on tracing paper, using a soft, dark pencil.*

2 *Transfer the motifs to acetate film and go over them to mark the outlines clearly.*

3 *With a fine, sharp scalpel, cut carefully around the outlines.*

4 *Place the stencil firmly on the surface and fill the shape with colour using a stencilling brush.*

Start with simple designs, without cutting out large areas of the stencil board. If too much rigidity is lost, you will find that it is difficult to manage the stencil while applying the finish. Indeed, as the patterns become more complex, bridges will be needed to keep the board stiff. Cut these bridges as thin as possible, as the unpainted areas will need to be touched up after stencilling.

Multi-coloured patterns are produced by using a number of stencils. The important thing is to make sure all the stencils are compatible. Do so by punching holes in the corners of each board, then line the holes up with marks on the original drawing or tracing. The holes can also be used as references when applying the finish.

Applying the finish

The groundwork for stencilling can be any colour or material – but for walls a matt undercoat or eggshell is best, though emulsion works well. The advantage of water-based paints is that they dry fast; although that does not matter for the background, it is vital when colouring the stencil shapes. Stencils are generally applied on a light or pastel background, but there is no reason why the pattern should not be picked out in bright colours against a darker background. On wooden objects, seal the piece first with matt varnish (gloss has less key) or a sanding sealer.

The position of the pattern is important, so try it out first, marking off reference lines along the edges with

Stencilling a chest of drawers using a ready-cut stencil
◀ **1** *Painted furniture is a common recipient for stencilling, though natural wood can also provide an excellent background for subtle patterns and colours.*

Make sure the painted piece is thoroughly prepared before application, using an undercoat as a base. The undercoat does not have to be white – pastel colours are the best alternative.

▶ **2** *For these small patterns, on a painted surface, use artists' colours mixed in shallow dishes. Test the colour on white paper. Position the stencil and tape it down firmly. Apply the colour by dabbing with a stencil brush. Press down hard on the stencil, and do not use too much paint, to ensure that none of the material creeps under the stencil. Sharp lines are essential.*

CHOOSING STENCIL DESIGNS

● Stencilling can be used on almost any surface, from walls, floors and ceilings to small boxes. The ability to produce repetitive designs is one of its most obvious features; stencilled borders are therefore particularly popular. Equally, single identical motifs on a series of doors or drawers can look most effective.

● Floral and ribbon designs are widely available, and can easily be copied from pictures or even wallpaper. Use a photocopier to enlarge or reduce a design to suit the requirements of a particular piece. Geometric shapes work well as borders, or as rug patterns on floors; and a twisted rope effect can be achieved with proprietary stencils or by cutting out a series of leaf shapes. Look at woven or printed designs on rugs, curtains, wallpaper and linen for ideas and tracings.

● Try to use a stencil that is appropriate for the piece. Animals always look good on toyboxes and on cupboard doors. A string of camels, like a frieze, around a child's room is fun, as are almost any well-defined animals. Children's books are a good source for designs, but animal stencils are sold by most craft shops and by some stationers and toyshops. Fruit and other everyday objects are equally suitable and especially rewarding for children, who can pick out the different images. A sequence of shapes can be made to look more interesting if no one image is painted in a particular colour more than once.

● As far as possible, blend the shape of the design to the shape of the piece or area being decorated. The idea is to enhance the piece, not to impose an unsuitable image that confuses the eye. However, there is plenty of opportunity for imaginative stencilling. For instance, the silhouette of a window can be stencilled on a floor to create the illusion of sun streaming into the room.

▲ **3** *Once the first colour has started to dry, remove the stencil. Try to avoid dragging the colour, as it will be difficult to touch up. Leave the motif to dry.*

▲ **4** *Apply a second colour by dabbing with the stencil brush.*

◀ **5** *Select the next motif to be applied, and mix up a suitable colour. Make sure that the colours match, and that enough is mixed to complete the stencilling – mixed colours are difficult to repeat.*

chalk. This can easily be wiped off later – but you must remember to do so, as a coat of varnish would seal the lines in forever. Do not start applying the stencil before the background is completely dry; similarly, never add further stencil colours until the previous one is dry.

The best means of applying the paint is with a special stencilling brush. These are not expensive and have short bristles shaped rather like those of a shaving brush. Use the stencilling brush with a dabbing action, as if stippling (see pages 86–89). First, though, you need to attach the stencil to the workpiece, making sure the board fits as snugly against the surface as possible. Any gaps will allow the paint to creep, producing a poorly defined and untidy finish. When applying the paint, have an instrument such as a paint scraper ready for pressing down the stencil in place, using your spare hand.

Mix the colour to suit, using artists' colours in an oil paint or glaze. Mix sufficient for the job, as it will be

▶ 6 *Three colours have now been applied, and the pattern is taking shape. Notice how the stalks of the flowers are a dark colour, and the emphasis is given to the flowers or seed pods, which are brighter.*

▼ 8 *Stencilling is particularly effective for brightening up a nursery, bathroom or kitchen. Any combination of colours can be used, but always make sure each application is dry before attempting the next, and keep the stencil clean at all times.*

▲ 7 *Use a simple repetitive pattern to join up the more detailed shapes. This livens up the piece, without making it fussy. Try to follow the shape of the piece being stencilled;* highlight edges, corners, door panels and drawers. Stencils can have a number of patterns cut in them, but too many make the stencil weak.

difficult to reproduce the exact colour later (see pages 66–69). Do not make the paint too thin, or it will run. Decant a small quantity of the finish onto a palette of some sort (glass works well). This helps to keep the amount of paint on the brush to a minimum, and so also reduces the chance of creep.

After painting the pattern, leave the stencil in place for at least 30 seconds and then remove vertically in one action. This may need some practice. Wipe off any excess from the stencil, using white spirit, before applying more paint. This is why acetate or oiled board is so good. When creating a repetitive pattern, make sure that the board does not disturb the previous motif as you move on. Sometimes the board will have to overlap; in which case wait until the paint is dry, and in the meantime work on another area. It is important to have marked out the position of each pattern with chalk before starting. Try to keep the spacings and borders regular.

Coordinating stencils
▲ *Although these stencils are both simple two-colour patterns they brighten up surfaces by following the line of the* *stairs and by picking out the drawer fronts on the chest.*

Combining decorative techniques
▶ *Before stencilling, this shelf unit was rag-rolled to give the background a garden feel. The eye is drawn towards the two painted plant pots, but notice how the repetitive patterns above the shelves and along the leading edges balance the design.*

HINTS AND TIPS

● Special marking pens are needed for drawing on acetate.

● Bevel the edges of board when cutting out shapes. This reduces the likelihood of creep.

● Attach tracings to board with masking tape.

● Keep stencil clean.

● Try out patterns with coloured paper shapes first, or with paint on scrap material.

● Do not use absorbent material for stencils.

● Apply the paint lightly, with a dabbing action.

Wait until the pattern is dry before applying another layer or a protective coat of gloss or matt varnish. One effect worth trying is a single coat of matt varnish over two coats of gloss. This softens the glossiness a little. Use stronger, two-part acid-catalyst varnishes for floors, but make sure before application that they do not react with the colours.

"Antique stencils"
▼ *This sideboard has been painted, though some of the wood's grain has been allowed to show through. This effect is enhanced by the light patterns on the rails and end panel.*

USING COLOUR FOR STENCILLING

● When stencilling, you are attempting to produce an overall effect – so make sure the colours used are compatible. Do not use too many colours, as that means cutting or buying more stencils. Floral stencils often look best in pastel shades, while silhouettes and geometric patterns generally benefit from strong contrasting colours.

● Try also to keep the stencilling sympathetic to the piece. Old items may need faded colours, to suit their age, while modern furniture with hard lines can take stronger colours and bold decoration. When applying a stencil pattern to wood, bear in mind the colour and figure of the grain. Stains will let the grain show through but tend to creep and to spread rapidly, though pigment-suspension stains can solve the problem.

Repetitive stencilling
▼ *This is a fine example of repetitive stencilling. The floorboards have been given a thin wash. The larger pattern has been stencilled in a darker shade and the smaller stencil is picked out in a more contrasting white. Notice how the faults and holes in the floorboards complement the repetition of the stencil, softening its effect.*

111

Crackle finishes

Crackle finishes are used for two quite distinct reasons. The first is to age a piece, simulating the cracking of finish over the years. Alternatively, an interesting decorative effect can be created with contrasting colours. This is sometimes used for imitating leather. In both cases, a coat of crackle glaze (a clear glaze available from finishing suppliers) is applied to the piece. As the glaze dries, surface tensions are produced, causing the finish to craze. It is possible to apply this finish by spraying (see pages 148–149), but the technique and materials used are different.

Apply a coat of oil varnish. Leave until tacky then apply the glaze to the surface with a flat brush, laying it on the surface, without working it at all, as the cracking will appear at once.

To highlight the effect, once the glaze is dry, rub wax polish into the cracks, using a soft cloth, then lightly burnish the surface. Alternatively, brush a thin scumble (see pages 86-87) into the cracks and wipe off the excess. You can either buy the scumble ready-mixed or mix your own, using gold size, pigment and white spirit. Once the surface is dry, burnish with a soft cloth. Crackle glaze needs no further protection – in fact, coating it with varnish would be pointless since that would cover up the cracks.

Coloured crackle finish

For a decorative effect, apply a coloured crackle glaze over a contrasting colour. Experiment with combinations of colour and shade. First, apply the coloured "undercoat", making sure the surface is smooth. Then mix the second colour with the crackle glaze and apply it to the dry surface; as the glaze cracks, thin lines of undercoat will appear.

The best effects are created with complementary colours – for instance, red and black or blue and red. Some colours look best as the top coat; others, especially the brighter colours, work better underneath. Lime green with gold cracks looks good, as does dark maroon with gold cracks, black with white, and gold with silver. Try all sorts of combination. Mix the background colour with standard glaze, and apply it to the prepared surface with a brush. As with the clear crackle glaze, seal the wood with shellac sanding sealer first.

For an antique gilt effect, apply a silver background and cover it with a clear glaze tinted slightly with brown. Once the crackle has dried, rub dark-brown scumble or wax into the cracks. This works well for gilt picture frames, which often crack with age – either because the original finish was low in resins and substance or because oil is buried below layers of French polish.

HINTS AND TIPS

● Always test effect on scrap board of similar consistency.

● Make enough coloured glaze to finish the job.

● Let each coat dry before applying the next one.

● Do not skimp on preparation.

CRACKLE PATTERNS

● Small boxes take a crackle finish well, whereas a dining table is probably too big. When applying a crackle finish to large items, lay the crackle glaze on heavier and wetter than for small pieces, in order to produce a generous "crazy paving" pattern.
● It is important to create a crackle finish that suits the piece. Never exceed 50mm (2in), even on large areas, as the finish can start to peel if the pattern is too wide. On rails and slender frames, a 6mm (¼in) pattern looks best.

A selection of different crackle finishes

▲**1** *White background and pink crackle.*

2 *Brown background and pink crackle.*

3 *Dark green background and yellow crackle.*

4 *Yellow background and turquoise crackle.*

5 *Black background, and blue crackle.*

MEMO

❖

Tools and materials
Flat brush

Oil varnish

Undercoat or eggshell paint

Wax polish and pigment

Artists' oil colours

Crackle glaze

❖

Common problems
Uneven application produces an uneven pattern.

Too much colour will make the finish too dark.

❖

Drying time
Let shellac sealer dry for 15 minutes.

Glaze takes about 30 minutes to dry, but leave longer.

Leave crackle glaze to dry for 1 hour.

Applying a crackle finish

▲**1** *The crackle is going to be used to age a mirror frame. In other circumstances crackle works for decorative effect. Make sure the surface is thoroughly prepared. In this case, the frame has been wiped with white spirit.*

▲**3** *When the varnish is tacky apply a coat of crackle glaze. This is supplied ready for use. The size of the crazy paving pattern produced depends on how much glaze is applied. A thicker coat results in a wider crackle. As with the varnish, lay on the glaze, allowing it to flow freely.*

▼**4** *As the glaze dries ι cracks, producing the distinctive pattern. This can be enhanced by rubbing the cracks with dyes or pigmented wax, which can be made to contrast or complement the undercoat colour.*

▲**2** *Having prepared the surface, and masked off any areas that do not need to be cracked, apply a coat of oil varnish. Do this with a flat brush, laying it on so that there are no brush marks.*

Distressing

Distressing, also known as antiquing or faking, is used to "age" contemporary furniture or new components of antique pieces. The simplest guide is to look at furniture of the relevant period and try to imitate the markings.

When preparing the surface, bruises and knocks can of course be ignored – but do not be tempted to ignore machining marks, which will betray the youth of the piece. The distressing is done with hard objects, such as bags of nuts and bolts, bicycle chains and hammers, often softened by cloth. Water marks can be reproduced by using a cup with stain smeared on the bottom. When distressing, make sure the marks are deep enough to break the fibres thoroughly, so they will take plenty of water stain. This makes the dents look even darker, as if they have collected dirt over the years.

Without holding back on distressing the surface as a whole, concentrate on the areas likely to suffer with time. Legs get bashed regularly, as do edges and table tops. A small bag of nuts and bolts works particularly well and helps create a random pattern of bruising. Mass-produced reproduction furniture often exhibits distressing that looks too systematic, since it follows a pattern, having been done by machine. Try to keep the effect as natural as possible, and practise first on some scrap wood or even on a rejected piece of furniture that is beyond repair.

Distressing to imitate age
▼ *A mahogany panel straight off the production line (left) is deliberately aged with colour, dents and marks (below). The moulding around the edge has been battered, as would happen to a vulnerable section of a piece over time. The bruises and ring mark on the top are subtle as if they too have blended into the dulled finish. This panel can now sit more comfortably in a room full of antiques.*

◀ **1** *Use a bag of nuts and bolts to make bruises and dents on the surface. The contents need to be heavy enough to do some damage. Make sure you move the bag around in a random motion; mass-produced reproduction furniture can be identified by a regular pattern. Concentrate on edges and legs.*

MEMO

❖

Tools and materials
Colour mops

Metal objects

Polishing rubber

Soft cloth

Stains

Transparent polish

Wax polish

❖

Common problems
The distressing pattern will not look natural if it is too regular.

Do not distress an existing finish. Pieces must be stripped back first.

❖

Appropriate surfaces
Any piece can be given an antique finish. However, an antique or distressed finish is obviously inappropriate for contemporary furniture.

❖

Drying time
Water stain takes about 40 minutes to dry.

▶ **2** *Once the surface has been distressed, apply a water stain. Use plenty of stain, keeping it wet as you manipulate it around the piece. Rub the stain into the damaged fibres of bruises and dents so that they show up darker.*

▲ **3** *When the stain has dried, seal the surface with a shellac sealer. Wipe the sealer across the surface with a soft cloth, using straight strokes along the grain.*

The idea is to seal in the stain, and not to build up a finish. Ensure that the coat of sealer is even.

▲ **4** *Many old pieces have ring marks, from alcohol on glasses or hot water under cups and mugs. To imitate such a mark, fill a metal container*

with hot water and wet the bottom. Leave this on the surface for five to ten minutes to make a dark ring.

115

▶ **5** *Stain is not sufficient to give the piece a colour that reproduces the effects of ageing. Mix spirit stains and pigments with polish in a boat, and apply with a mop brush. Cover the whole surface liberally with colour and rub into the wood, to produce a darker finish. Try to produce a slightly opaque colour mix.*

◀ **6** *After the colour has dried, apply a coat of transparent polish using the polishing rubber. Work up a body until a finish just short of full grain has been produced. Start with a circular pattern, moving across the surface. Finish with straight strokes following the grain.*

▶ **7** *An antique piece will have lost some of the shine of new polish, so dull the surface once the polish has dried. Use fine 000 wire wool to rub the polish with straight strokes along the grain. Finish with a coat of dark coloured wax polish to enhance the aged appearance.*

Finishing distressed furniture

Once you are satisfied with the distressing, stain the piece dark then wipe off the surplus. The stain will bite into the marks, making them show up dark, as old marks would. Use water stain, as it gives you plenty of time to fiddle around with the finish. Leave any odd splashes to simulate splashed marks made over the years – but rub the stain off the corners and mouldings, as would happen with time. Seal with a shellac sealer.

Lightly sand the dried stain with fine abrasive (see pages 18–21) and begin the polishing process with transparent polish, which tends to make the surface look faded (a tinted polish would liven it up and make it look newer). Work up to a semi-filled finish, with the pores partly filled, but do not try to produce a high gloss. Dull this finish using 000 grade wire wool, rubbing evenly in the direction of the grain. Finally, apply a tinted wax with a soft cloth, before burnishing. Or use a dulling brush and pumice powder, sprinkling the surface with the powder and sweeping the brush with the grain, then polish with wax.

Corner cabinet with distressed finish
▲ *Andy Holmes' corner cabinet, made from recycled materials, is a fine example of how marks and dents give a piece age.*

Combining distressing and coloured wash
◄ *A combination of distressing and a coloured wash give this chest of drawers a feeling of age. Particular attention has been paid to the vulnerable parts of the piece, especially the edge moulding.*

Rubbed finishes

HINTS AND TIPS

● Remove the
stain gradually, by
rubbing in
progressive
stages.

● Do not make
sharp lines – the
rubbed effect
must blend in
subtly.

● Make sure the
surface is smooth
at each stage.

● Damp down
before starting to
polish or apply
stain.

A rubbed finish is used to simulate the effects of age on a piece of furniture or panelling, by rubbing stain selectively to produce the highlights and dark patches of wear. The technique is most commonly used on oak reproduction furniture, particularly reproduction Jacobean items, but it can be used on other timbers too.

Start by preparing the surface in the normal way – though, since the aim is to achieve an antique feel, it will look more convincing if you leave some of the blemishes and bruises. Which faults you leave will depend on the degree of distressing (see pages 114–117) you hope to accomplish. But make sure any conspicuous machining marks are removed, as a genuine antique piece would be unlikely to exhibit the telltale ripples produced by a power planer!

Stain the piece using Vandyke crystals mixed with water, to create a dark colour. Water stains are available by mail order from finishing specialists, see back of book for some useful addresses.

Once the stain has dried, sand lightly to remove any roughness. Then overstain, using a dark solvent wood dye. Work the stain into the grain, but leave corners and mouldings unwiped, so that they are darker than the rest. Leave to dry before rubbing.

Using 000 grade wire wool, make a pad to fit in the hand. Work on the highlights until the dark stain has been rubbed off, then continue rubbing until the patchy effect has been subtly blended in and there are no definite lines remaining between the light and dark areas. On panels, rub the centre,

easing the colour off without making a sharp line. Always work in the direction of the grain, gradually easing the colour. Once the desired effect has been achieved, clear the shreds of wire wool and wood dust from the surface.

The idea is to remove the finish from those areas that over the years would be worn away by wear and tear. The tops of beads on mouldings and the edges and corners of chairs and tables are, for example, particularly liable to wear. Conversely, more inaccessible areas collect dust and dirt, and so darken with age. To simulate that effect, mix pigments and spirit dyes with polish and touch up the low points (around raised panels, on inside corners, and anywhere out of everyday reach), using a mop. Take a good look at old woodwork to see how it ages.

Use a dark garnet polish for finishing the rubbed effect. Apply at first with a soft cloth, and then leave to dry. Sand, using fine paper (about 320 grit), then dust off and continue to apply polish with a rubber (see page 58). Shade in any parts that show up too distinctively, using a spirit colour with small amounts of pigment, applied either with a soft cloth or colour mop. If a deeper finish is required, use white polish as a final coat. Leave to dry and continue polishing, but do not build up a high-gloss finish, which would be inappropriate on antique furniture.

Once the polish has dried, use 000 wire wool to dull the finish, to create a satin or semi-matt effect, always following the grain. After dulling, apply a wax finish with a soft cloth, using a pale coloured wax polish. Finish off by lightly burnishing.

Producing a rubbed finish

▲ 1 Pieces such as this mahogany stool acquire rubs with age. After years of use, the colour is no longer even — lighter areas appear at the centre of panels, on seats or chair backs.

▲ 2 Prepare the stool to produce a smooth surface and then apply colour. In this case a dark water stain (Vandyke) is used; it penetrates well, and can be worked into corners and crevices to give a darker colour. Rub the stain into the mouldings.

▲ 3 Once the stool has been stained, wipe off the surplus and leave to dry. Then sand lightly and overstain using dark solvent wood dye. Note the darker areas on legs and corners.

▲ 4 When the piece is dry, rub off the stain with fine 000 wire wool or flexible abrasive (as here). Start from the centre of a rail or panel and work towards the corners. Rub off more stain in the centre than in the corners, blending gradually towards them.

Use spirit dyes, mixed with polish and applied with a colour mop, to enhance the rubbed effect. A dark solvent wood dye will help the contrast, but make sure the colour blends in. Use a dark garnet polish for finishing the rubbed effect.

▲ 5 Give the finished stool a coat of white polish, working up to a semi-full gloss finish. Then wax polish the piece, to bring out the colour and add depth. Distressing at an early stage will enhance the impression of age.

119

Liming

The principle of liming is similar to that of grain filling (see pages 53–55). It is used on open-grained timbers (most commonly oak), a liming paste being worked into the pores of the wood. When the surface is fully finished, liming enhances the grain pattern, by emphasizing the pores and leaving a contrasting colour.

Although it is possible to make your own liming paste, buying a tin of liming paste is worthwhile in the long run. Proprietary pastes include drying agents, which speed up the process.

If you want to colour the paste, decant a quantity into a shallow container (never contaminate the paste in the tin with colour). It may be difficult to repeat the colour – so mix plenty for the task. Most coloured limed finishes are pastel shades (pink and green are popular choices), so avoid making the paste too dark.

Open the grain with a stiff wire brush, working in the direction of the grain. If you need to stain the piece, use a water stain, before liming, and seal with a shellac sealer. Leave

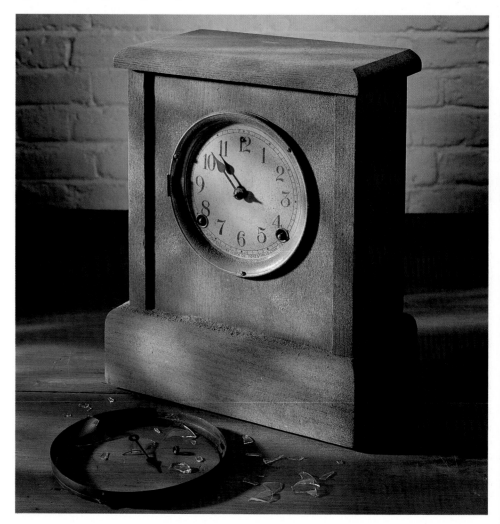

Producing a limed finish

▶ **1** *An oak clock case, which has been chemically stripped of previous finishes ready for liming. Oak is particularly appropriate for liming because of its open grain, but other timbers can also be used.*

▲ **2** *Take off any fittings, and sand the piece with 240 grade abrasive paper. Check all the surfaces to ensure that they are free from dirt and grease.*

▲ **4** *After opening the grain, stain the piece with any colour. It is best not to use solvent wood dye because this can* cause patchiness at a later stage. Leave the stain to dry.

▲ **3** *Open up the grain to take the liming paste by rubbing the surface with a stiff wire brush, using straight strokes along the grain. Try to open the grain evenly, and not more deeply in some areas than in others. Check the results* regularly against the light, making sure the whole surface has been worked with the wire brush.

▲ **5** *Seal the stain with a pale or white polish to ensure the liming paste does not dry patchy. If a harder, more durable finish is required seal the* stain or the bare wood with teak oil or even a coat of varnish that has been thinned with white spirit.

MEMO

❖

Tools and materials
Scrapers and abrasive for preparing the surface

Hessian and soft cloth

Liming paste

Water stain

Dyes and pigments

Shellac sealer

Wax

Wire brush

❖

Common problems
Do not colour the paste too darkly.

If liming paste is applied in the direction of the grain, it will not fill the pores consistently.

❖

Appropriate surfaces
Open-grained timbers, especially oak, also elm and ash.

Kitchen furniture and fittings, panelling, staircases and restored furniture.

❖

Drying time
Leave liming paste to dry overnight before finishing off.

overnight to ensure that the sealer is thoroughly dry and hard before rubbing in the lime paste – otherwise the stain can be worked away, resulting in a patchy effect.

Rub in the paste with hessian, working across the grain. If you work in the direction of the grain, the paste will not hold as well in the pores. Do not use too much paste at any one time. After letting it dry for about 10 minutes, gently wipe off the excess, working in the direction of the grain.

Then leave overnight before applying further finishes.

On oak, a wax finish is most appropriate. There is no reason why other finishes cannot be used – but rub carefully with the polishing rubber if applying French polish, so that none of the liming paste is raised from the grain.

▲ **6** *When the polish has dried it will have sealed in the stain. The liming paste needs to be rubbed in, which would affect the stain if it was not sealed.*

◄ **8** *Liming paste is a combination of wax and white pigments, and is supplied ready-mixed. Apply the paste with a cloth, before rubbing it into the pores using a piece of hessian. Work across the grain. White undercoat or white gloss can be used instead of liming paste. Wipe across the grain, making sure all the pores are filled and the surplus wiped off across the grain with a rag dampened with white spirit.*

▲ **7** *Smooth the sealed surface with a flexible abrasive, or use fine 320 grade abrasive paper.*

▼ **9** *Before the paste dries, wipe off any excess with hessian, across the grain. Make sure the grain is filled evenly, and that not too much is wiped off.*

◀ **10** *Gently wipe with the grain to remove any cross-grain marks that were made by the first wiping session. Do not wipe any of the paste from the grain.*

A selection of liming effects
▶ **1** *Spirit blue stain and limed.*
2 *Natural oak colour and limed.*
3 *Red pigment-suspension stain and limed.*
4 *Spirit green stain and limed.*
5 *Red and yellow pigment-suspension stain and limed.*

▶ **11** *Leave the paste to dry overnight and then burnish the surface with a soft cloth. Apply a coat of white or pale polish to seal the paste. Do not use too much polish, but allow the natural sheen of the wood to show through.*

5

Spray finishes

Modern finishes can be as attractive as traditional ones, and often as much skill is needed to apply them. The scope and range is as wide and varied, and the preparation of the surface with abrasives, fillers and stains every bit as important. Sophisticated machinery is used in factories for the application of finishes, but home woodworkers and small workshops need little extra equipment for modern finishing

Spray guns and the spray workshop

HINTS AND TIPS

● Always select a good quality spray-gun. Buy the best one you can afford.

● Try out the gun to see how it feels.

● Always clean out after use, making sure the holes are not blocked.

● Lubricate all parts with general-use oil.

The principal feature that distinguishes the various types of spray gun is the way the finish is held and then passed to the nozzle for atomizing with compressed air. There are basically only three options – and unless bulk spraying with a pressure-feed gun is required, the choice is really limited to gravity-feed and suction-feed guns. For small jobs such as stencilling the range can be extended to aerosols, but they are rarely used by professional finishers except for touching up damaged spray finishes on site.

Convenience, economy and the types of finish to be used are the criteria to consider when choosing a spray gun. For the small workshop, gravity-feed guns are normally the most convenient. They are easy to handle, economical (as small quantities can be mixed for short jobs), and suitable for most finishes.

Suction-feed guns are less convenient, as the underslung reservoir makes them unwieldy. However, they only need small quantities of finish at a time; and they are the most popular option when using heavy pigmented finishes for spraying cars and other metallic surfaces.

Each of these guns (with perhaps the exception of aerosols) produces the smooth finish associated with spraying, so long as they are maintained properly (see page 135) and the materials and workpiece are thoroughly prepared. Aerosols are more difficult to use, because they cannot be adjusted and the material is not atomized as consistently.

Gravity-feed guns

Most woodworkers wanting to kit up their workshop for spraying are likely to buy a gravity-feed spray system. If, on the other hand, you are mainly going to spray metal with coloured paints, then you will probably choose the suction variety. Gravity guns are simple and easy to use. The finish is

CHOOSING A SET-UP

● Each gun can be adapted to suit the needs of differing finishes by changing the set-up of air cap, nozzle and needle. These are supplied in various shapes and sizes, with all sorts of hole configurations in the air cap. Each component is marked with a code, and manufacturers publish a chart to show which air cap should be used with which nozzle and needle for any particular finish. It is important to use the correct combination of parts.

● Tell your supplier what finishes you expect to be spraying. The chances are that you will be able to use one versatile set-up for all wood finishes, but you may need a special air cap and nozzle for high viscosity finishes such as polyester and filling primers. Needles are usually standard, but check that you have one that is suitable.

● The viscosity of a finish affects the set-up you choose. High viscosity finishes require a larger set-up.

● Stains and polyurethanes have the lowest viscosity; and nitrocellulose the highest, though this depends on how much thinner is used (in order to produce a thin or thick coat). Whenever possible, use two thin applications rather than one heavy coat.

Spread adjuster
This regulates the quantity of air flowing out of the horn holes in the cap and so changes the shape of the fan.

Needle adjuster
The needle restricts the amount of fluid flowing out of the gun.

Air cap
Air is blown through small holes in the air cap, atomizing the finish.

Trigger
Squeezing the trigger opens the air valve and draws a needle away from the nozzle to release the fluid.

Handle
Handle for gripping gun.

Air flow adjuster
This is adjusted to suit the material being sprayed – higher for thicker materials, lower for thin materials.

Cup
The cup stores the finish, and is carried below the gun.

A suction-feed spray gun
▲ *This type of gun is recommended for spraying heavy pigmented finishes.*

Cup
The cup stores the finish and screws into the top of the gun.

Spread adjuster
This regulates the quantity of air flowing out of the horn holes in the cap and so changes the shape of the fan.

Air flow adjuster
This is adjusted to suit the material being sprayed – higher for thicker materials, lower for thin materials.

Needle adjuster
The needle restricts the amount of fluid flowing out of the gun.

Air cap
Air is blown through small holes in the air cap, atomizing the finish.

Handle
Handle for gripping gun.

Trigger
Squeezing the trigger opens the air valve and draws a needle away from the nozzle to release the fluid.

A gravity-feed gun
▲ *This gun is probably the best piece of equipment for anyone taking up spray finishing.*

mixed and stored in a cup that screws onto the top of the gun. The cup takes about 550ml (1pt), which is ample for spraying both sides of a 2m (6ft) table top with one coat of finish.

It is important not to run out of material midway through spraying a large surface such as a table top. Spray finishes dry within minutes and the gun must be kept on the move all the time, so trying to spray a surface in stages can result in a patchy finish. There are few wood-finishing operations that will use up a full cup in one go – but always err on the side of generosity when measuring finish, so you do not run out at a critical moment. Equally, do not overfill the cup on a gravity-feed gun, as it can then spill finish over the piece as you spray, leaving conspicuous droplets that take time to flatten with abrasive.

When assembling the spray gun, make sure that the small plastic filter at the bottom of the cup is in place, to stop dirt getting into the gun and blocking the nozzle. In use, the finish flows down into the gun and out of the nozzle. There the finish is atomized by air blown through small holes (called atomizing holes) in the air cap, which surrounds the nozzle, and through the horn holes that stand proud on each side of the air cap.

With the compressor working, the gun is constantly ready; but the compressed air will only flow when the trigger is squeezed. Squeezing the trigger opens the air valve and draws the needle away from the nozzle to let the finish out. However, the initial pressure on the trigger opens the air valve only a little, without allowing the finish to flow, thus ensuring that material does not drip out of the gun onto the workpiece without being atomized.

The beauty of the gravity-feed gun is that it is so easy to use. The cup does not get in the way as you spray, and you can work with small quantities of finish at a time. If you are planning a long session of spraying with stain, mix plenty of stain in a larger container, as you will not be able to repeat the colour exactly. Gravity-feed guns are susceptible to clogging and slow flow when spraying heavy paints because of their high solid content, especially those that produce a metallic effect. Suction-feed guns are better for such work, but are generally not as convenient to use.

Suction-feed guns

Suction-feed spray guns are broadly similar to gravity-feed types, but the finish is siphoned up from a canister slung below the gun. The nozzle of a suction-fed gun protrudes further through the air cap than on gravity-feed or pressure-feed guns. As the air rushes out through the air cap, a vacuum is formed that sucks up the finish from the reservoir. Adjustments are much the same as on the other guns, though the set-up of nozzle, needle and air cap is different.

One advantage of suction guns is that the reservoir can be larger than on a gravity gun. You therefore don't have to refill it as frequently, which saves time. It also helps when mixing the finish. As the canister holds that much more, mixing up in another container may be unnecessary. However, the size of the canister and the fact that it is often made of metal (rather than plastic as for gravity-feed guns) does make the gun heavy. Also, if you lose concentration, the canister tends to hit the surface and mark the finish.

Another advantage is that you can mix the finish in the canister before attaching it to the gun (whereas on a gravity gun the cup has to be screwed in place before it can be filled, which is less convenient). When fitting the canister to the gun, make sure the filter at the bottom of the pipe is in place.

When you look at a suction gun, you will notice that the pipe that picks up the finish from the canister is bent. This is a design feature. When the gun is tipped forwards, as often happens while spraying, the pipe needs to point towards the front of the canister, to ensure that it sucks up finish and not air. If air is sucked up, then the finish is likely to be uneven.

Why suction-feed guns are particularly suitable for spraying finishes with a high solid content, such as metallic paints, is that heavy particles of finish tend to sink to the bottom of the reservoir, where they will not be sucked up – whereas they would be the first to drop into the workings of a gravity-feed gun, slowing the flow or even blocking it up. Suction guns are, in fact, equally suitable for thin-flow coats. These are used when a thin final coat of finish is needed that will flow smoothly across the surface. They may have as much as 15 per cent thinners content.

Compressors

For efficient spraying, air must be supplied to the gun at a constant pressure. It is also vital that the air is clean and dry. These requirements are achieved by two items of equipment: a compressor and an air regulator.

When buying a compressor, the specifications to look for are the volume of air supplied and the maximum pressure that the compressor is capable of providing. Spray-gun manufacturers produce set-ups of air cap, needle and nozzle to suit any air supply from 0.2 to 0.6 cubic metres (6 to 20 cubic feet) per minute. For first-time buyers, they

recommend a compressor that supplies 0.3 cubic metres (12 cubic feet) per minute at 4 bars (60lb psi) pressure.

Once you have chosen a compressor, tell the spray-equipment supplier which kind you have selected and they will offer a set-up to suit your system.

Compressors work by drawing air through a filter and pumping it, under pressure to a receiver tank, to the air regulator. The pump can be driven by a diesel or electric motor, but the cheaper ones plug into the mains and are much easier to maintain. The air regulator which needs to be as near to the spray booth as possible, regulates the air pressure and extracts any moisture or oil. It incorporates a series of filters, and a meter to measure and adjust the air pressure.

While compressors can be bought or hired relatively cheaply from many manufacturers, it is best to purchase an air regulator from a spray-equipment supplier. It is important to buy a reliable one that will ensure a steady flow of compressed air. When you are spraying, there's nothing worse than a fluctuating air supply. If the air supply falters, the gun will splutter momentarily and will fail to atomize the material, allowing drops to fall on the surface.

A drainage tap on the air regulator

SPRAY GUNS AND THE SPRAY WORKSHOP

provides an outlet for collected moisture. Before each spraying session, open the tap to let out any water – otherwise it may percolate through to the gun and cause the finish to be ruined. (see pages 164–167).

There is also a drainage tap on the compressor's receiver tank. When the compressor has been turned off, open this tap and let the water drain out (water tends to build up in the tank because air heats up and condenses it as it is subjected to pressure). The armature of the pump can burn out if it has to run against too much pressure – so if you are doing a long run of spraying, turn off the compressor at lunch time and drain the tank before resuming work.

Organizing a spray workshop

Very little equipment is needed in a spraying workshop – indeed, the less clutter the better, as it only collects dust. There are, however, a few important accessories that aid successful spraying; and, as in any finishing workshop, natural north light makes it so much easier to check the surface thoroughly.

Turntables and pin boards

For the spray booth (see page 132), buy or make a turntable on which the piece to be sprayed can stand or lie. If you have a swivel chair that is beyond repair, you can make a turntable by salvaging the swivel mechanism and placing a platform on top. It is useful to be able to adjust the height, and to have larger platforms for bigger pieces. Thin sticks of wood help to raise the piece off the turntable and reduce the likelihood of marking the finish. Longer, thicker battens can be used to extend the table.

Another way to support workpieces without marking them is to make a pin board. This resembles a fakir's bed of nails. Take a piece of ply and drive nails through it so that the points protrude by 12mm (½in), spacing the nails at 75mm (3in) intervals.

Drying racks

Especially in a cramped workshop, drying racks are handy for stacking panels. You can also hang chairs from these racks, spacing the arms further apart than the standard 20–25cm (4–6in) gaps. Make a homemade rack, using 50 × 50mm (2 × 2in) timber, with long feet to which uprights are joined by angle brackets. Use dowelling for the arms, fixing them into holes drilled in the uprights.

Cleaning facilities and materials

Make sure there are cleaning facilities in the workshop. This does not mean you need a drain – in fact, never pour waste finishes or cleaning material into the main drains. Keep a sealable metal container for waste materials, and take it to an approved site for disposal. Spray-gun manufacturers provide special brushes for cleaning spraying equipment, but a good supply of rags is useful too.

Cellulose thinners will clean all modern finishes, so always have plenty to hand. They can be bought in large quantities – but, rather than continually opening large containers, decant thinners and finish into smaller more manageable bottles, using a funnel.

Spray-gun brackets

Once spray guns have been cleaned, they need to be hung up out of the way. There are special brackets available from gun suppliers, shaped like bicycle clips but sturdier and wider, into which the guns fit after cleaning and while in use. Take care when using full gravity-feed guns, as they sometimes tip back in these brackets, allowing the finish to leak out of the top. Most guns are produced with hooks worked into the body, in which case you can use a nail or cup hook instead of a bracket.

Spraying tints

You will need a selection of spraying tints, which are based on cellulose and can be mixed with any modern finish for colour matching or special effects. Red, black, green and yellow are sufficient to start with.

Spray booths

The environment for spraying needs to be free from dust. It must also be well ventilated, as the solvents and atomized solids used for spraying are harmful and need to be kept away from the finisher.

Factories have sealed booths that provide a dedicated spraying area, with powerful extractor fans to clear the air in the booth of dangerous fumes. The solids are filtered off by water or fibre filters, so that only the solvents are blown out into the open air. Few woodworkers, however, can afford the space or expense of an industrial spray booth.

Homemade spray booths

One possibility is to erect a homemade spray booth in your workshop. It can be any size to suit your work, and does not necessarily have to be sealed. In fact, many industrial spray booths are open on one side. You can build a small booth with a simple 50 × 50mm (2 × 2in) timber framework clad with thin plywood. Cut a hole in the back of the booth, and fit an extractor or fan to extract the fumes from finishing materials and expel them from the workshop. Cover the hole with a fibrous filter to catch solids. If the filter clogs up periodically (layers of gauze are often used), that means it is working satisfactorily.

Line the sides of the booth with paper, so you can simply strip it off and replace it when it gets coated with finish. It's vital to keep booths and spraying workshops clean – as dust, besides marring sprayed finishes, is also a fire hazard. Dampen the floor to trap dust. Since the extractor in your spray booth will draw dust towards it, it is important to keep the whole area clean.

When using a booth, never spray with the gun pointing away from the extractor – otherwise the spray will be diverted away from the area you are aiming at and may cover you instead. A revolving stand for the workpiece is therefore essential in a spray booth, so the piece can be turned and you don't have to move round it. You can either buy a turntable, as used by sculptors and potters, or make one of your own (see previous page).

Adjusting and using a spray gun

There are four adjustments to any type of spray gun. However, the air flow adjuster normally stays fully open all the time, as it is much easier to alter air pressure at the air regulator (see pages 130–131), where there is a gauge. This is useful for adjusting the size of the particles borne in the air flow. Most finishes run at 2bars (30 to 35lb psi), but by cutting the pressure right back splattering effects (see pages 144–145) can be achieved.

The fan adjuster (also called the spread adjuster) is much more important, as it regulates the quantity of air flowing out of the horn holes in the cap and so changes the shape of the stream. With this valve fully open, the flow is a very flat ellipse. The flow returns to a funnel shape about 50mm (2in) wide when the air is cut off from the horn holes. Use a wide ellipse (as wide as the gun will allow) for flat surfaces. A more cylindrical flow is needed for rails, legs and narrow surfaces.

It is also possible to adjust the fluid flow carrying the finish. This is done by limiting the travel of the trigger, which restricts the needle's movement away from the nozzle. Close up the fluid adjuster for finishes that have been thinned for easy flow; open it up for heavy pigmented finishes. You know that too much material is being applied if runs appear on the surface.

The final adjustment is to direct the fan of finish vertically or horizontally.

Adjusting a spray gun
◄ **1** *Adjusting the needle travel to alter the flow of material from the gun.*

▲ **2** *Unscrew the knurled knob to allow more material out of the gun, and tighten to restrict the flow.*

▲ **3** *Test the flow of material through the gun, and keep adjusting the needle stop until the required flow is achieved. Spray a piece of scrap as a test. If the coat is heavy and runs, too much material is being used. If the surface does not look wet, not enough lacquer is passing from the nozzle.*

CLEANING A GUN

● Proper maintenance of a spray gun is essential. It will not work efficiently if any of the tiny air and fluid holes are even slightly blocked – and as modern spraying finishes dry very fast, this can happen quickly. Smooth results may be jeopardized by foreign bodies in the spray gun; and, especially if you use more than one type of finish for spraying, consistency of colour is likely to be marred by any residue left in the reservoir.

● Immediately after spraying is completed, pour any finish that remains in the cup into a waste container, for disposal at a toxic-waste disposal point. It is not advisable to pour the residue back into a can containing fresh finish, as that may contaminate it. This is certainly true of any material mixed with a catalyst or thinners, but you may find that there is no adverse effect on finishes that are used straight from the can.

● Clean all parts of the gun with thinners, paying special attention to the holes in the air cap and nozzle. It is not necessary to remove the nozzle, but take off the air cap and clean it thoroughly. Use a brush to clean the inside of the gun; and make sure that all holes are clear. Do not leave the gun to soak in thinners overnight, as the packing may shrink and dirty solvent can block vital air passages. After cleaning, reassemble the gun and oil all moving parts.

With the horn holes horizontal, the fan will be vertical. Most of the time you will be spraying from side to side, and so want the finish to be directed in a vertical swathe, as if you were painting with a flat brush. You will therefore only need to alter the setting when you are going to spray up and down.

Using a spray gun

Modern finishes are popular not only for their qualities of resistance, but also because they can be applied consistently at an economic rate. Indeed, a professional spray finisher will say that a consistent finish is the most important characteristic of a job done well. Some practice is needed in order to fully understand the formula for a fine finish and to learn the hand-to-eye coordination required when working with a spray gun. Even so, you will be surprised how easy and quick it is to get started – and you will soon appreciate the potential of a spraying system.

The important variables to experiment with are the fluid, spread and air-supply adjustments on the gun and air regulator, and the viscosity of finish being used. There is no benefit to be gained from high air pressure, as high pressure makes the air and atomized finish bounce back onto the finisher – so keep the pressure as low as possible, without creating globules of finish. About 2 bars (30lb psi) is sufficient for most finishes. If the flow of fluid is too fast, you will be unable to keep up and the finish will start to run. Always use two or more thin applications, rather than one thick coat.

The distance between the gun and the surface, together with the smoothness of the sweep as you are spraying, is critical for the finish. This is where the skill of the finisher really tells. Generally, unless the manufacturer of the finish recommends otherwise, spray with the gun about 20cm (8in) from the surface. Too near will result in runs; too far spreads the finish too wide.

Keeping the spray consistent

Consistent spraying is accomplished with smooth, steady sweeps of the gun, parallel to the surface. When learning to spray, there is an almost irresistible tendency to keep the wrist firm, as if putting in golf. When putting, the arms form an arc, with the hands further from the ground at the beginning and end of each stroke than at the moment when the club hits the ball. So, if you keep your wrist rigid when spraying, the part of the work closest to you will receive a thick coat of finish (often with runs), whereas the areas furthest away from you will be more thinly coated.

The trick is to flex your wrist as your arm moves. Try not to move your body unless absolutely necessary. If you move your body, that will upset the consistency of the sweep – so keep your body still and only move your

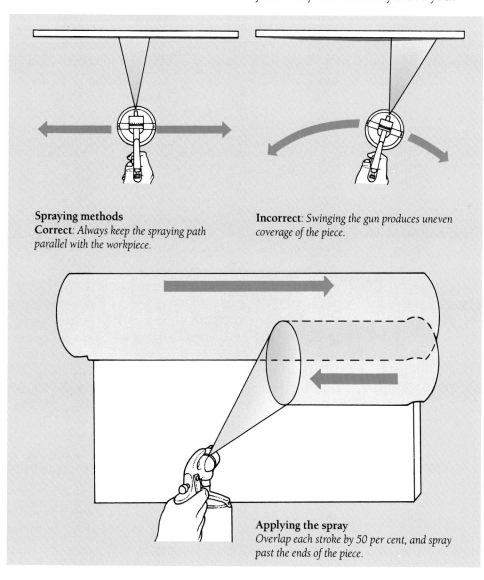

Spraying methods
Correct: *Always keep the spraying path parallel with the workpiece.*

Incorrect: *Swinging the gun produces uneven coverage of the piece.*

Applying the spray
Overlap each stroke by 50 per cent, and spray past the ends of the piece.

HINTS AND TIPS

● Test colours by spraying them on scrap wood (if possible, similar to the timber of the workpiece), to get a true idea of the finish.

● Always spray parallel to the surface, flexing the wrist and keeping the gun an even distance from the workpiece. Most finishes should be sprayed about 20cm (8in) from the surface.

● Keep the air pressure as low as possible, and the fluid flow at a rate you can keep up with.

● On wide surfaces, overlap each sweep of the gun by about 50 per cent.

● Continue each sweep beyond the end of the piece to ensure complete coverage.

arms. The aim is to keep the spray gun parallel with the surface all the time. Flex your wrist as if ironing a pair of trousers or painting a door.

Spraying a table

When you are spraying, there is always going to be some overspray that does not hit the desired spot. Most will be sucked out by the extraction system, but some of this material is bound to fall upon areas already finished. Do not, however, be frightened to overspray at the end of each sweep, and do not be tempted to take the pressure off the trigger. A constant flow of finish is vital, even if, momentarily, the gun is not aimed at the surface. It is important to start and end each sweep with the spray at full blast. Do not alter the flow with the trigger. Instead, adjust the gun. Always spray with the trigger full on. To ensure an even coat across a wide surface, such as a table top, overlap each sweep by about 50 per cent.

Because some of the overspray will always fall on finished components, leave the most visible parts till last and start with the most inconspicuous areas. On a table, that means spraying the inside of the legs or underframe first, and then the outside. When it

comes to the table top, always spray the edges first, even though they are more obvious to the eye than the underneath. This is because more overspray is created when spraying the edges than when working on the bottom or top. After the edges, spray the bottom and, finally, the top.

Finishing with spray is rather like veneering. If only one side is sprayed, it may "cup" (distort) due to the pull of the drying finish. So always finish both sides, even if the top is fixed in place.

Spraying a chair

Before starting to spray, check the spread adjustment on the gun. Test this by spraying on a piece of scrap or against the side of the booth (see page 132). A wide fan, which is ideal for spraying a table top, would produce too much overspray on the rails and legs of a chair. So reduce the amount of air channelled to the horn holes; and spray in a cone-shaped fan, spreading to about 50mm (2in) as it hits the surface.

It does not matter how you spray rounded chair legs and rails, but try not to point the spray gun directly at the face of square components. Instead, position the gun so that it is aiming at an edge and two faces. This way you can spray both faces simultaneously, which saves time and consumes less finish. However, do not use this method when spraying components wider than about 40mm (1 ½in), as that may result in an uneven finish.

When spraying a chair, start with the legs. Spray the inside of a leg first, then the outside. Spray the rails in the same manner. Next, spray the outside (i.e. back) of the chair's backrest, then the front of the backrest, and last of all the seat.

Aiming a spray gun
When spraying a curved chair leg, spray directly at the centre of the piece, using a narrow fan shape. For square-shaped legs, direct the spray at the corners of the piece, again with a narrow fan shape.

Types of spray finishes and their application

In this section we look at how to prepare surfaces to take spray finishes, then we look at specific spray finishes and their application.

Preparing surfaces for spraying

When it comes to preparing the surface for spraying, the usual rules for producing a smooth, blemish-free surface apply. Unless an alternative method is recommended, all the spray finishes described here are compatible with the various stoppers, grain fillers, waxes, stains and sealers used for non-spray finishes.

Use shellac or two-part stoppers where appropriate (the latter are recommended for larger repairs). Cellulose waxes are handy for filling small holes, while either oil-bound or resin-bound fillers should be used for a full-grain finish. It can be used between coats of cellulose finish to fill dents that have been missed during preparation.

Solvent wood dyes should not be used for staining pieces that are to be sprayed. Catalysed finishes in particular are likely to react with these stains, changing the colour of the timber radically. A dark oak, for example, may suddenly turn rose red.

Water and spirit stains can be used under spray finishes, though before applying a water stain, remember to raise the grain by damping the timber then sanding it flat. Spirit stains can be sprayed on, though the results are unlikely to be superior to application by hand.

Sealing and colour matching

Most timber will need to be sealed before the first spray coat. The type of sealer varies from finish to finish, and

Stripping a chair for spraying
◀ **1** *The gloss finish on this chair needs to be stripped off before preparing to spray. It is quicker to strip with chemicals rather than trying to cut back the old finish using abrasives.*

137

▲ **2** *Always wear protective gloves, overalls and goggles when working with chemical strippers.*

Decant a little stripper at a time into a metal paint kettle. Ventilate the workshop or work outside.

▲ **3** *Using a flat brush, lay the stripper onto the surface, keeping it wet as it is applied. Do not brush it around – this will only speed up*

evaporation and reduce the effectiveness of the stripper.

▲ **4** *Use a paint scraper to test to see if the old finish is ready to be scraped off. Always scrape with the grain.*

Remember to wrap waste scrapings in newspaper, and dispose of them carefully.

▶ **5** *Use a bunch of coarse wire wool to rub off any of the finish that is left on the surface. Always wear heavy gloves when working with this grade of wire wool, and do not try to tear it from the roll – instead, cut it with shears or a pair of old scissors.*

▶ **7** *The finished chair, ready for sanding through the grades with garnet paper, from coarse to fine.*

◀ **6** *Apply another coat of stripper, and rub off waste with more coarse wire wool, using a stick or spatula to remove finish from nooks and crannies. Do not use a metal point because it is likely to scratch the wood. Check the manufacturer's instructions to see if the stripper needs to be neutralized. Follow their instructions for doing so.*

138

can be determined by the timber type. Once the first spray coat has been applied, some colour matching may be necessary. In all cases this can be done using spirit dyes, either mixed into lacquer and sprayed onto the workpiece or simply rubbed on. The alcohol base will bite into all spray finishes, even acid catalyst.

Alternatively use spray tints, which are sold in tins of 500cc (1pt) upwards, ready-mixed with cellulose, though they can be further diluted with the appropriate finish. Sometimes called cellulose colours, they are powerful – so use them in small quantities. Apply more than one tint to obtain the right match, spraying on and leaving to dry for about 5 minutes. They are the most suitable option for shading (see pages 146–147), for which they are best used after the first sealer coat.

How many coats?

Depending on the effect or protection required, one or two coats of finish will be sufficient. It varies from one piece to another. An average-size kitchen-table top will need about 700cc (1¼pt) for spraying both sides with one coat of finish, while a chair will need about 500cc (1pt).

Spray finishes dry quickly (within 20 minutes), but take longer to cure. It is important to apply the second coat as soon as possible after the first – once the surface is touch dry and has been lightly sanded (denibbed) – so that it can bite in before the curing process starts.

Burnishing

Although they are available in matt or gloss, you may want to boost the gloss of spray finishes further. Use rubbing compound and a burnishing mop attached to a drill. Last of all, buff by

Staining with a spray gun

◄ **1** *Spirit stains can be sprayed, though rubbing stain in by hand is likely to produce a superior result. Use a gravity-feed spray gun to apply the stain. This type of gun is the easiest to handle around the chair. Regulate the pressure at 1.3bars (20lb psi), and apply a wet, even coat. Work from the inside of the legs outwards. Then stain the edges and the underneath of the seat before starting work on the top. The idea is to stain the most visible areas last.*

◄ **2** *Wipe off any surplus stain using a clean cloth until an even colour has been achieved. Leave to dry.*

HINTS AND TIPS

- A makeshift spray booth can be erected from polyethylene sheeting, but make sure it is well ventilated.

- Check filters regularly for clogging.

hand with burnishing cream and a soft cloth.

Nitrocellulose finishes

Nitrocellulose is the oldest of modern spray finishes. It was first used at the beginning of this century as "dope" to stretch and strengthen the canvas covering of early aeroplanes. It was favoured for its quick-drying qualities. The cellulose compound, which remains a base ingredient of many spray finishes, is extracted from the cotton plant.

Nitrocellulose finishes are about the simplest to spray, as they are used directly from the can, without having to mix them with catalyst or thinners. Only add thinners to NC finishes when they are not atomizing properly – and even then they should be thinned by no more than 10 per cent. Globules of finish on the surface are evidence of the lacquer being too thick.

Before spraying, seal the timber by hand with a shellac sealer and leave it to dry for 30 minutes before lightly sanding with fine silicon-carbide paper. There are also various sanding sealers available with a lacquer base, which include an agent to make sanding easier. However, this sanding agent is a soapy material and may create problems with adhesion of subsequent coats of finish, so try it out first. Sanding sealers can be used on open-grained woods such as oak, ash and elm.

Other sealers are available, too, which suppliers recommend for particular finishes. If you are not sure which to choose, ask the manufacturer for a compatible finish and sealer. Polyurethane and shellac-sealers are good for oily timbers, followed by any other finish, and also for refinishing when there is a risk of silicones in the grain. Do not use more than one coat of any sealer.

Having sealed and denibbed the surface, spray the first coat of NC. Leave this to dry for about 20 minutes before sanding it and applying the next coat. However, it takes 2 or 3 hours before NC is ready for burnishing. For a quick cheap finish one coat of NC is sufficient,

Spraying on sealer

▶ **1** *Use a gravity-feed spray gun to apply the sealer. Set the pressure at 1.5bars (25lb psi). Apply an even coat, making sure that all areas are covered. Again, work from the least visible towards the conspicuous parts. Do not apply too heavy a coat – this is only meant to be a sealing application.*

▶ **2** *Leave the sealer to dry for about 20 minutes at 18°C (65°F). The surface is then slightly rough and will need smoothing. Use fine 320 grade self-lubricating silicon-carbide abrasive paper, always following the grain and taking care not to break through the sealer and stain. Be especially gentle on the corners, and hold the paper flat in the hand, with the centre two fingers pressing it down onto the surface.*

but a thin-flow coat on top adds depth and strength.

Acid-catalyst finishes

The main drawback to AC finishes is that they have to be mixed with a catalyst, which adds to the setting up time. The acid catalyst needs to be handled carefully, wearing protective gloves. AC finishes have been in use for about 40 years, and are supplied with either a melamine-formaldehyde or urea-formaldehyde base in matt or gloss. Their great advantage is that they are hard-wearing, being especially popular for table tops.

However, their power does have detrimental effects upon stains and some timbers. Brown oil stains are often turned red by AC finishes, and red streaks are sometimes produced in sycamore and certain fruit woods, such as pear. Acid-catalyst finishes are also sensitive to silicones and waxes on the surface, so use a detergent to clean the piece before spraying and preferably seal with a shellac sealer when refinishing old wood. Make sure any stain is completely dry before applying the finish (a dry surface will look matt). Follow the recommended drying times on the side of the stain bottle.

Resin-bound grain fillers are the most compatible with AC; oil-bound fillers should be avoided. Acid-catalyst finishes have a high solid content, so will fill the grain to a greater extent than other spraying lacquers.

When spraying AC, try not to apply it as wet and thick as other finishes. Turn down the flow rate slightly, and sweep a little faster with the gun. Always use two coats of AC. The proportion of catalyst to base varies from manufacturer to manufacturer. However, adding more catalyst than recommended does not speed up the curing time and will produce a brittle finish; it is also more likely to react with stains. If you use too little catalyst, then the finish will not cure at all. So always follow the instructions provided with the finish.

Because AC has a high solid content, it may be necessary to thin it, with thinners recommended for AC finishes. This helps produce a more flowing coat.

An acid-catalyst finish takes ½–1½ hours to dry, depending on the room temperature, and can be recoated as soon as it is touch dry. The hardness of

Spraying colour and lacquer
◄ 1 *Once the sealer has dried, lightly sand the chair and then wipe off any dust. There will be parts of the chair, particularly the highlights, that need to be touched up with colour. Turn the pressure right down to 1bar (15lb psi) for touching up.*

▶ **2** *Picking out the lighter areas, gradually build up an even colour. Do not try to use too much colour in one pass. Work from front to back, finishing with the back slats. The back usually needs more colour than any other part of the chair. Unlike any other spraying operation, touching up the colour may require more spray in some areas than others.*

▶ **3** *After the final application of colour, apply gloss lacquer. Turn the pressure up to 1.5bars (25lb psi), and plan your route around the chair. Start inside the legs, moving on to the slats, and finishing with the seat. Always spray the most important surfaces last.*

the coating increases over a period of about seven days; the harder the lacquer the easier it is to burnish. Therefore wait at least 24 hours before burnishing. If the article you are finishing is a table, use table mats for the first seven days and wipe off any water spills immediately.

Paint finishes

Nitrocellulose and acid-catalyst finishes are available in paint form for special effects, such as splatter, and also for simple painted surfaces. Contrary to the expectations of woodworkers hoping to hide the defects of their work, paints highlight errors more than any other finish. A black finish is perhaps the most difficult to produce and the least forgiving. Preparation has to be faultless; and, where possible, it pays to spray paints on medium-density fibreboard, which is smooth and requires no filling.

Use an NC or AC pigmented finish for interiors, and polyurethane for outdoors. When grain-filling, which is often necessary, use an oil-bound filler before spraying with NC; otherwise, use either an oil-bound or resin-bound grain filler and any stopper.

Once the surface is perfect, apply an undercoat. Finishing suppliers sell special undercoats, which are cheaper than thinning down the finish coat and are specifically formulated to aid adhesion. Leave the undercoat to dry for about an hour, then flat down with fine silicon-carbide paper. Make sure the surface is thoroughly dusted down, as the smallest speck or hair will show up later. Apply the finishing coat, in either gloss or matt. If necessary, spray on further coats before burnishing.

◀ **4** *The finished chair has an even glow.*

Water-borne finishes

With most spray finishes, the solid element is carried from the gun to the surface by a petroleum-based solvent, which then evaporates. In some cases, the solvent comprises as much as 70 per cent of the finish. It therefore made sense to try to discover a solvent that was inexpensive and environmentally harmless. The answer was water.

Unlike most spray finishes, water-borne finishes do not liven up the surface; and, although they are available in gloss form if required, they have a flatter, more natural appearance than other lacquers. As a result, they are a common choice for Scandinavian-style pine products. You can buy water-borne finishes in either one-part or two-part form. In the latter type, a cross-linker is used as the hardener. Follow the manufacturer's instructions for mixing this catalyst with the bulk of the finish. Store water-borne finishes in a frost-free cupboard.

If staining is needed, use water stains (not solvent wood dyes). Before applying water stains, raise the grain then sand.

A water-borne sealer should be used prior to spraying. Before applying the sealer, dampen the surface to raise the grain, then let it dry and sand it lightly. Do not use a grain filler when working with water-borne finishes, as adhesion is not always satisfactory. After sealing, do any colour matching that may be needed, using spray tints or spirit dyes.

When spraying, turn the fluid rate down. Most solvents evaporate to some degree between the gun and the surface, but this is not the case with water-borne finishes – so try to use thin coats and keep the viscosity up, in order to avoid runs.

Water-borne finishes are not compatible with other spray finishes. The gun and other equipment must therefore be absolutely clean before use, otherwise the finish is likely to foam.

The final coat can be left as it is or rubbed with 000 wire wool and wax. Rub in the direction of the grain, with even strokes, to produce a satin finish.

Creating special spray effects

Spraying, as a means of applying finish, has been the product of an industry striving for efficiency. Today, spray guns are fitted to automated machinery and run like robots controlled by computers. Moreover, the potential for a more artistic approach has not been lost on professional finishers and illustrators. The airbrush, which is favoured by graphic designers for much of their creative work, is simply a miniaturized version of the spray system found in woodworking workshops.

Although the standard spray gun does not offer the accuracy of an airbrush, there is ample scope for producing special effects. These effects fall into two groups: those that are determined by special materials, and those that require creative use of the gun and its adjustments. In both cases, it is possible to achieve similar effects by hand – but, with practice, you will find spraying quicker.

Splatter finishes

Splatter finishes are among the easiest of creative spray effects to produce. By hand, surfaces can be splattered with a toothbrush, creating an irregular speckled pattern. The same results can be achieved in the spraying shop, by adjusting the air pressure, fluttering the trigger, and altering the distance between gun and surface.

When using a spray gun, globules of finish are dropped onto the surface by

Applying a splatter finish
◀ **1** *Turn down the air pressure at the air regulator until it is just sufficient to atomize the finish. Test the effects of this on a piece of scrap, or the side of the spray booth. The finish must not be mixed too thinly, otherwise it will continue to atomize without forming the characteristic splatter globules.*

▲ **2** *Patchiness is not always a disadvantage when splattering. If you want an even splatter, keep the gun moving all the time. Vary the distance of the gun from the work surface to alter the size of the splatter globules. The nearer the gun is to the piece, the larger the blobs of finish.*

turning down the air pressure at the air regulator. This means that, instead of the finish being atomized into a thin spray, the material falls on the workpiece in droplets. Pastel colours are normally best for the background, with brighter splattering on top. There are no strict rules to follow, and you may find other colour combinations suit the situation better. Choose colours that complement each other.

Any type of paint or pigmented finishes, which are available from finishing suppliers, can be used for the base coat and for splattering. Make sure the surface is thoroughly prepared. Apply one layer of undercoat and then the required base, sanding with fine abrasive between coats.

Fill the spray gun canister with splatter finish mixed to the same viscosity as the base coat. Turn down the air pressure at the air regulator until it is just sufficient to atomize the finish (test this on some scrap). By pulling back the trigger further, more

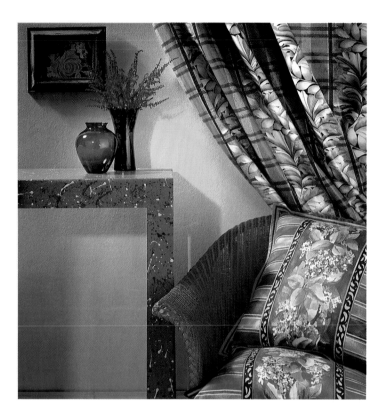

material will flow to the nozzle, creating a thicker splatter pattern. The closer the gun is to the surface, the bigger the speckles will be, as the particles of finish break up in the air.

Once you are satisfied with the effect (and there is no reason why further coats of splatter in different colours cannot be added), protect the surface with one coat of matt nitrocellulose finish. The splatter for this final application should dry almost immediately – but leave for an hour or so, just in case.

Shading

While either suction or gravity-feed guns can be used for a splattered finish, the latter are best for shading, as they are much easier to manipulate when trying to replicate the aged look produced by rubbing (see pages 118–119). Though it may take time to develop the skills necessary for accurate shading (especially, creating

Combining colours
▲ *This painted side table shows some of the extreme effects that can be produced with a sprayed splatter finish. Not only have three or more colours been used, but the distance between gun and workpiece has been constantly changed to create a range of globule sizes. Some have become so large that they have distorted so that they look like rockets in flight.*

▲ **3** *The finished panel shows fine blue speckles on a white background. Light colours are best for the background, but* *there are no limitations to the number, size and colour of the splatter marks.*

darker areas in corners and recesses), you will find that gradual shading of a panel from the centre outwards is as easy as by hand.

Stain the piece using a water or spirit stain. Stain to the colour required for the lightest areas. Seal this with a shellac sealer, then sand gently with 320 grit silicon-carbide paper and dust off.

Use spray tints for the shading. Mix to a colour about half a shade darker than the original stain. The trick is to use a tint that is not too dark, otherwise it becomes very difficult to produce gradual shading from light to dark. The aim is to avoid any sharp definition between shaded and unshaded areas. Darken those areas that are most likely to collect dust with

age, building up the colour in recesses and internal corners with coats of spray tint. Finish with a matt NC lacquer.

Sunburst effects

You may be excused for mistaking sunburst for shading. The effect is similar, though sunburst is used for decoration as opposed to reproduction and restoration. It is popular on guitars, car dashboards and wooden surfaces that have to blend in with plastic and metal. It is a flamboyant finish, and some artistic flair is needed in order to achieve an attractive result. Stunning effects can be produced with bright yellow, greens, and reds; or more subtle effects with browns and wood colours.

Spraying a sunburst finish

▼ **1** *Guitars and dashboards are the most common objects for a sunburst, or shaded finish. Make sure the surface is flat and smooth before starting the spraying operation, removing any blemishes where necessary.*

▲ **2** *Use fine self-lubricating silicon-carbide abrasive paper for the final sanding.*

Always sand with the grain, holding the paper flat in the hand.

◄ **5** Build up the shading, blending it with the lighter areas. Although the aim is to produce a darker ring around the edges, it is important that there is no obvious line between dark and light. Build up the shading slowly, rather than applying a single, heavy coat.

▲ **3** Apply the base stain, using a spraying or spirit stain. Choose a colour that is lighter than the finished colour required. Keep the coat as even as possible. If you have a choice of spray guns, use a gravity-feed type for this operation.

◄ **6** Protect the sunburst effect with two even coats of clear lacquer. Denib between applications. Dashboards are often sprayed with a high-gloss finish, but it is equally appropriate to use satin or matt lacquers.

▲ **4** Start applying the darker, shading spray gradually building up the colour from the outer edges of the guitar. The principle of producing the brightest areas in the centre of panels is true for the majority of pieces.

◄ **7** The finished guitar, showing the gradual shading from light to dark. In this case, the sunburst finish has been used as decoration, but it can also be used to imitate the rubbed quality of older pieces.

147

Once the surface is flat and has been thoroughly prepared, stain with a light colour, in spirit or water form (see pages 44–49). Seal the stain in, using a sanding sealer (see pages 44–49), and leave to dry before sanding lightly with 320 grit paper. Clean off any dust. Select a spray tint a little darker than the stain and spray outwards from the centre, as if shading.

· Now choose an even darker tint and shade the outer edges. Leave to dry for an hour or so, then spray on a protective coat of NC lacquer – or acid-catalyst lacquer if the piece is likely to be subjected to wear and tear.

Hammer finish

The reason a hammer finish is so named is not because a blunt instrument is used to distress the surface, but because the finish resembles hammered pewter or metal. It is a special effect used to make surfaces look metallic. Like wrinkle, it hides the grain of the piece. It can be used perfectly well on elaborately grained timber – but it is a pity to hide the character of an attractive wood, and medium-density fibreboard is probably the best substance on which to work.

A hammered finish is produced by two spraying applications. The first coat is a cellulose spray based on an aluminium paste, to give the metallic content. Once this has been applied, on a thoroughly prepared surface, leave for 5 to 10 minutes; then apply a splattered coat of ethyl acetate (the appropriate solvent) at low pressure, to break up the aluminium and create the hammered look. The lower the pressure – for example, 0.5 bar (5lb – 10lb psi) – the wider the hammered pattern will be. Higher pressure – about 1 bar (10–15lb psi) – produces a tighter effect. Use the air regulator to

regulate the pressure.

Some skill is required to produce a hammered finish, because the distance of the spray gun from the surface is another factor that determines the degree of hammer. With the gun close to the workpiece, the splatter will be wider. Try to keep the distance constant, so you produce a consistent hammer effect.

Hammer finish is sold in a variety of colours, and can be mixed with spray tints. Blues, reds, yellows and greens are all popular colours for a hammer effect. Although it is possible to mix your own hammer finish in the workshop, it is more realistic to purchase it ready-made. However, it is expensive and for that reason it is mainly used for small items.

Remember when preparing the surface that you are trying to achieve a metallic effect, so the surface needs to be exceptionally smooth. If necessary, protect with NC or AC spray once the finish is dry, which takes about 2 hours.

Before and after hammer finish
▲ *An oval panel before and after spraying with a hammer finish, which in this case imitates pewter. The effect is produced by a combination of two spray applications. The second coat is sprayed on when the first is still tacky.*

148

Crackle finish

A sprayed crackle finish is produced in much the same way as by hand, the effect depending largely on the heaviness of the coat. A thick wet application results in a wider pattern. The resins in the crackle are described as "underbound". This means that there is not a sufficient solid content to cover the surface – so, as the solvents evaporate, the solids are drawn together, forming a crazed pattern.

Having prepared the surface, spray or brush on an undercoat and flatten with fine abrasive, ready for the base coat. This background colour will be seen through the cracks of the pattern, so you need to work out in advance what colours are compatible. Mix small quantities of the base and crackle to test the colours. Green and gold work well together, as do gold and silver, white and black, and blue and red. Contrasting colours work best, though subtle shades can be equally effective.

Leave the base coat for about an hour, or until dry, before applying the crackle. Add spray tints to the crackle to produce the desired colour. It is possible to make up your own crackle, rather than buy it ready-made. Use dry pigment to suit, together with 2 to 3 per cent resin and a cellulose base, plus a solvent (such as ethyl acetate) to thin the crackle for spraying. Start by buying proprietary crackle from a finishing supplier, then progress to homemade finishes once you are familiar with the finish.

Before spraying, turn down the air pressure to about 1 bar (15psi). The cracks form almost immediately, as the crackle hits the surface and the solvents evaporate. The background colour breaks through the cracks. As with hand-applied crackle glaze, the heavier and wetter the coat the bigger the pattern. Vary the size to suit the piece. A large table top will need a 50mm (2in) crackle pattern, while rails and small items need a pattern no more than 25mm (1in) wide.

Finally, spray the crackle with either a gloss or matt nitrocellulose lacquer, then leave it to dry for about 10 to 15 minutes.

Before and after crackle finish
▼ *This old shelf unit has been sprayed with a crackle finish to give it more colour and a feeling of age. This particular crackle effect was produced using a white background colour oversprayed with blue crackle glaze and a matt cellulose coat.*

6

Guide to woods

The aim of finishing is to bring out the best in wood,

enhancing the grain and colour, while protecting the

surface. It is therefore important to understand

wood, and learn to identify the most common

species. With that knowledge you will be able to

apply the most appropriate finish for any

particular type of wood

Introduction

Timbers are customarily divided into two groups, hardwoods and softwoods. This classification has a botanical basis. Softwoods have narrow leaves, whereas hardwoods have broad leaves. There is also a difference in wood structure between the two groups. From the woodworking point of view, hardwoods are generally denser and harder than softwoods – but there are exceptions. Balsa (*Ochroma*), for example, which is classified as a hardwood, is one of the lightest and softest woods there is.

The role of finishing in conservation

In addition to the differences between softwoods and hardwoods, and between heartwood and sapwood, timber displays a great deal of variation in terms of colour, texture, grain and pattern – each species having its own characteristics and its own particular uses.

In the past this diversity was taken for granted, but nowadays there is increasing awareness that timber cannot be used at the present rate without irreparable damage to the world's rainforests and grave consequences for the entire environment. Unfortunately, the highly figured hardwoods – traditionally the most highly prized timbers used for fine woodwork – are the very ones that are in danger of becoming exhausted. However, by using the appropriate finishes it is possible to upgrade the appearance of timbers that are not threatened, and to use them in place of endangered exotic woods.

Substitutes for exotic timbers

In the following pages, some of the woods that are most popular with finishers are described in greater detail, together with recipes for traditional and modern finishes. Included are suggestions for ways to finish sustainable timbers to resemble exotic woods, so the reader will be able to avoid using timber species that are becoming depleted.

Commercial hardwoods

Oak (*Quercus* spp)
One of the most widely available timbers. Its many uses include furniture, boatbuilding and flooring. Harder types are found in England, Western Europe, North America and Japan. Other varieties are grown in Australia and central Europe.

Mahogany (Principally, *Swietenia*, *Khaya* and *Melia*)
Warm brown to red colour. Principally used for furniture, for making pianos and other musical instruments, and for woodcarving. Sources: Central and South America, and Africa.

Walnut (*Juglans* spp)
The colour and grain of walnut varies, depending on where it is grown. Uses include fine furniture, gun stocks, turning, woodcarving and veneers. Main sources: UK, France, Italy, Turkey, North America.

Teak (*Tectona grandis*)
Golden-brown in colour. A naturally oily wood, used for both interior and exterior joinery and furniture. Main sources: India and Burma.

Maple (*Acer* spp)
A close-grained timber, the colour ranges from white to light brown; the grain pattern varies from burr to straight grain. Uses include flooring and veneers for furniture. Main sources: Canada and USA.

Birch (*Betula* spp)
A close-grained, light-coloured timber. Uses include plywood manufacture and furniture. Sources: Europe and North America.

Beech (*Fagus* spp)
A close-grained, light-coloured timber. Steamed beech has a pinkish tone. Uses include cabinet-making, bentwood furniture and chair frames. Sources: Europe and North America.

Ash (*Fraxinus* spp)
An open-grained, light-coloured timber. Uses include furniture and tool handles. Sources: Europe and North America.

Elm (*Ulmus* spp)
A pale (sometimes pinkish) brown, open-grained timber. Uses include furniture, coffins, pit props and veneers. Availability has fluctuated because of Dutch Elm disease. Sources: Europe and North America.

Rosewood (*Dalbergia, Pterocarpus*)
A hard, purplish timber with dark figuring. Used for veneers and fine woodwork, and often for Victorian and Edwardian furniture. Now an endangered species. Main sources: India and Brazil.

Sycamore (*Acer pseudoplatanus*)
A whitish fine-grained timber with a flash in the grain. Uses include furniture and veneers. Sources: Europe and USA.

Afrormosia (*Pericopsis elata*)
Similar to teak in grain and texture. The colour is sensitive to light and can turn almost black. Used for furniture and shop fittings, and often as a substitute for teak.

Makoré (*Tieghemella heckelii*, syn. *Mimusops heckelii*)
Brown with darker markings. Used as a substitute for rosewood. West African in origin.

Obeche (*Triplochiton scleroxylon*)
Yellowish in colour. Used for furniture, finished to resemble mahogany. There are several similar timbers, including agba (*Gossweilerodendron balsamiferum*), utile (*Entandrophragina utile*) and abura (*Mitragyna ciliata*). Source: West Africa.

Commercial softwoods

Pine
(*Pinus* spp)
Baltic, Scots, yellow, white, pitch and parana (*Araucaria angustifolia*) pines are all used for woodworking, the colours ranging from pinkish to white and yellowish tones. Traditionally used in the building trade, pine is now being increasingly used for furniture.

Douglas fir
(*Pseudotsuga menziesii*)
Red to yellow in colour. Used for furniture, panelling, joinery and building construction. Sources: North America and UK.

Western red cedar
(*Thuja plicata*)
A reddish-brown timber that weathers to a grey colour. Used for exterior woodwork, including cladding, and for interior panelling. Sources: North America, New Zealand and UK.

Oak

European oak

American red oak

Oak (*Quercus* spp) has been used by man for hundreds of years for many different purposes and in all sorts of places, ranging from churches, stately homes and castles to boats and ships. It is a tough, hard-wearing timber, with excellent woodworking properties.

Oak is prepared by straight sawing and quarter cutting. When this is done, it shows medullary rays running across the grain pattern. Quarter-cut European oak has particularly pronounced rays.

There are reputed to be over 200 different types of oak, which divide into two main groups – red oak and white oak. The white oaks are considered superior to the red, as they have a finer texture. Within this basic subdivision, differences occur due to variation in growth and climate.

TYPES OF OAK

European oak
This is the hardest of the oaks, and therefore tends to be harder to work. It is generally preferred for furniture making.

Yugoslavian and Austrian oak
These are softer and have a straighter grain pattern. They also have a smaller grain and take stains well.

American oak
Most of the oak from the USA is red, although white oak is grown in North America, too. More than a third of the timber produced in the USA is oak. American red oak is much underestimated, and with the right treatment can produce some attractive effects.

Pollard oak
Mainly grown in Europe, pollard oak is cultivated by removing unwanted shoots to limit branch formation. As the tree grows, the burrs produced by this drastic pruning are incorporated in the timber – resulting in some particularly interesting grain patterns when the wood is cut and sawn.

FINISHES FOR OAK

*O*ak lends itself to thin satin or matt finishes, and responds particularly well to waxing. It is often limed (see pages 120–123). Other open-grained timbers, such as ash and elm, can be finished in a similar way to oak.

A number of different terms for oak finishes are used in the wood-finishing trade – such as church oak, Flemish oak and mission oak. Treat these names with caution, as they mean different finishes to different people.

When using red oak, the red tint can be overcome by applying a weak wash of spirit green before proceeding with any other finish.

JACOBEAN OAK FINISH

Prepare the surface. Stain with Vandyke crystals mixed to a dark shade. Leave to dry.

Apply a dark oil stain, rubbing well into the grain. Leave to dry.

Apply a coat of French polish. Leave to dry.

Sand lightly, using 320 grit paper.

Wax the surface with an antique wax polish. After three applications, burnish with a soft cloth.

This will produce a very dark oak colour with a silky finish.

WEATHERED OAK FINISH

Prepare a mixture of soda and lime dissolved in water to a concentrated solution. (Try a builder's merchant for lime.)

Apply this to the grain using a grass brush. Leave to dry.

Lightly sand off the residue.

The surface can then be waxed, using a white wax polish, or finished with a matt nitrocellulose lacquer.

Mahogany

American mahogany

African mahogany

One of the earliest records of the use of mahogany (mainly *Swietenia, Khaya, Melia*) was by Sir Walter Raleigh, who stopped in Honduras for repairs to his ship. When Queen Elizabeth I visited him on his return, she noticed the new decking and remarked how beautiful it was. Raleigh ordered the deck to be removed and had a table made from it for the queen. This generated an interest in mahogany, which increased significantly in the eighteenth century when furniture-makers such as Sheraton, Chippendale and Hepplewhite used the wood with elegant effect.

Mahoganies come from several parts of the world – including the West Indies, Central and South America, South-East Asia and West Africa. The characteristics, which depend on the timber's origin, range from the hard, heavy mahogany grown in Cuba to the much softer wood found in Nigeria and other parts of West Africa. Mahogany is a favourite wood for pianos, and the deep-red variety used for the backs of guitars and violins and other stringed instruments is known as "fiddleback mahogany". Recently, Brazilian mahogany has become particularly popular; the colour varies from golden-brown to pale pink. But very pale mahoganies exist, too, including white mahogany from the eastern USA.

TYPES OF MAHOGANY

Plain
No surface markings.

Stripy figure
The surface is broken lengthwise by stripes of uniform width.

Mottled
The surface looks as if it is mottled, due to the growth of the timber.

Crotch
As the tree grows taller, the larger branches twist and the fibres pull against each other. This produces the most highly figured mahogany. The "crotch" is the fork formed where the branches stem from the trunk.

FINISHES FOR MAHOGANY

Mahogany has a rich colour and figure second to none, so should be finished using as little surface colouring as possible. Many furniture manufacturers use coats of colour unnecessarily, masking the natural figure and colour of the wood. Originally mahogany furniture was waxed or oiled, but in Victorian times French polishing became more fashionable. When staining mahogany, avoid reddening the colour too much – it is better to aim for a brown tone. As mahogany is an endangered timber, it should not be used indiscriminately. Instead, you can stain butternut (sometimes called white walnut) to a mahogany shade, using mahogany crystals dissolved in water.

GOLDEN-BROWN MAHOGANY FINISH

Prepare the surface.

Stain the timber, using bichromate of potash dissolved in water. Add 2 tablespoons to 0.5l (1pt) of water.

Leave to dry, then sand lightly with fine abrasive paper.

Apply a pale French polish. After bodying up, stiff off (i.e. conclude the polishing with straight strokes in the direction of the grain).

This will produce a golden-brown gloss finish.

FULL-GRAINED BROWN-MAHOGANY FINISH

Prepare the surface.

Stain, using 1 tablespoon of Vandyke crystals to 0.5l (1pt) of water. Apply and leave to dry.

Fill the grain, using a brown-mahogany grain filler. Leave to dry.

Body up, using a garnet polish. Finally, stiff off.

Walnut

English walnut

American walnut

The colour of walnut (*Juglans* spp) can range from a dark, almost black, heartwood to a pale-grey sapwood. It is possible to bleach the timber to a creamy colour (blonde walnut was all the rage in the 1920s and 1930s), which gives it a rather washed-out appearance. As walnut has such strength, it can be fashioned into attractive shapes – for example, highly figured chair frames, with the grain running through.

Walnut is often used in veneer form, since the irregular growth of the tree produces beautiful veneers. Burl veneer (also known as burr veneer) is formed where there are outgrowths from the trunk, which have intricately grained timber. Butt veneer comes from the stump (or "butt") of the tree. It is cut across the grain to reveal the distinctive twisting grain pattern.

TYPES OF WALNUT

American walnut
The native American walnut (often referred to simply as black walnut) has a distinctive black grain. A strong wood, it is used for gun stocks and aeroplane propellers.

English walnut
Has a strong dark figure and a fine greyish colour, with the dark streaks that are characteristic of walnut. It is now in short supply and is not much used.

French walnut
Has a fine wispy figure. It is used for furniture.

Italian walnut
Very like American walnut. It has a black figure and a fine grain.

Turkish walnut
Has developed its own characteristics, due to the climate. It produces some of the most sought-after veneers because of the highly figured grain patterns.

FINISHES FOR WALNUT

*B*ecause of the natural beauty of the wood, the traditional finish for walnut was a wax one. Indeed, since walnut has so many natural colours and attractive grain patterns, there is a feeling among finish designers and woodworkers that these should be preserved by using either satin or matt waxed or oiled finishes. However, although it is considered that a gloss finish detracts from the timber's appearance, it is sometimes necessary and can look just as attractive as a matt treatment.

TRADITIONAL WAX FINISH FOR WALNUT

Prepare the surface.

As walnut has such a close grain and is a hard timber, grain fillers are not necessary.

If there is a contrast between the sapwood and the heartwood, colour matching will be needed. Apply walnut crystals with a brush to stain the sapwood, leaving the heartwood its natural colour.

Leave to dry, then seal with shellac polish or a sealer. Use a colour mop and pencil brush to match the grain pattern.

Apply beeswax, either with a cloth or a flat brush, and leave overnight.

Apply a further coat of beeswax and burnish with a soft cloth.

FULL-GRAIN FINISH WITH A FULL GLOSS

Prepare the surface.

Stain as required, using walnut crystals. Leave to dry.

Apply grain filler as required. Leave to dry.

Sand lightly with 320 grit paper.

Apply a body of white polish. Work it up until the grain is completely filled. Leave to dry overnight.

Cut back, using 320 grit paper.

Apply a final coat of white polish. Stiff off, then leave to dry.

Teak

Teak

Teak (*Tectona grandis*) is a hard timber with good weathering properties. It is grown in Burma, India, Thailand, Malaysia and Zambia. The natural colour ranges from a golden yellow to a darker brown. Being naturally oily, it is suitable for decking on boats and other situations exposed to moisture. However, the oily nature of teak can cause problems for the finisher – such as poor adhesion, bubbling and, with some two-part finishes, curling.

FINISHES FOR TEAK

Before treating teak with any type of finish, other than an oil-based one, it is advisable to apply a shellac sealer. A thin matt finish displays the timber's natural characteristics to best advantage. The traditional way of finishing teak was to use several coats of linseed oil. Today, finishes such as teak or Danish oils and tung oil are available. These dry faster than linseed oil, are easier to apply, and provide a more durable finish. Alternatively, for a fine satin finish, you can treat teak with a polyurethane oil.

TRADITIONAL FINISH FOR TEAK

Apply teak or Danish oil (or linseed oil), rubbing it into the grain with a cloth. Leave it to dry.

Apply further coats of oil.

Sand with fine abrasive paper between coats.

Finish with 000 wire wool and more oil.

POLYURETHANE-OIL FINISH

Prepare the surface.

Apply a coat of polyurethane oil thinned by 10 per cent, using a soft cloth and rubbing the oil into the grain well. Leave to dry.

Cut back, using 320 grit abrasive paper.

Apply a further coat of polyurethane oil, either with a soft cloth or by spraying. Leave to dry.

Finish with 000 wire wool and more oil.

MATT FINISH FOR TEAK

Prepare the surface.

Apply a coat of shellac sealer. Leave to dry for 1 hour at 65°F (18°C).

Sand lightly with 320 grit paper.

Spray with a coat of acid-catalyst matt finish.

TIPS FOR TEAK

It is possible to use stains on teak, but they do not take well. When applying water stains, add 1 teaspoon of ammonia to 0.5l (1pt).

Use thin coats when finishing teak. A matt or satin finish is best.

For outside use, treat teak with an exterior-grade varnish.

Maple

Rock
maple

Soft
maple

Maple (*Acer* spp) is a native of North America. Its uses vary from furniture to flooring, and the colour ranges from white to light brown. Two varieties of maple are available as commercial timber. Rock maple (also known as sugar maple) is the harder of the two. Soft maple (also known as red maple) has a darker colour and is much easier to work. Bird's-eye maple, which makes a highly decorative veneer, is produced when growth buds form but fail to penetrate the bark. As a result, when the timber is cut, an attractive grain pattern, looking rather like watered silk, is revealed.

FINISHES FOR MAPLE

Because of its close grain, maple takes most finishes well. It can be treated with either a matt or gloss finish, as required. A grain filler is not needed.

MATT FINISH FOR MAPLE

Prepare the surface.

Apply a water stain, using 2 parts mahogany crystals to 1 part Vandyke crystals, then leave to dry.

Apply a coat of sanding sealer.

When dry, apply a coat of matt acid-catalysed lacquer.

This will produce a golden-brown matt finish useful for domestic furniture.

TRADITIONAL FINISH FOR A NATURAL COLOUR

Prepare the surface.

Apply a body of white polish. Leave to dry.

Sand lightly with 240 grit paper.

Apply a final coat of polish, and stiff off.

GLOSS SPRAY FINISH FOR MAPLE

Prepare the surface.

Apply a coat of sanding sealer. Leave to dry for half an hour at 65°F (18°C).

Sand lightly with 320 grit paper.

Spray with a coat of gloss nitrocellulose finish.

This produces a tough gloss finish.

TIPS FOR MAPLE

Staining maple with mahogany crystals produces a finish resembling cherry.

Other stains can be used, but maple has a good natural colour which needs no improvement.

If using two-part acid-catalyst finishes, apply a shellac or sanding sealer first, as the acid tends to redden the timber.

Birch

Yellow birch

European birch

Paper birch

A close-grained hardwood, birch (*Betula* spp) is native to both Europe and North America. The grain can be straight or swirling, or an attractive "water-grain" pattern. The heartwood is reddish-yellow, and the sapwood white. Birch is used for furniture, panelling and the production of plywood. It is sometimes finished to imitate other timbers

Sycamore (*Acer pseudoplatanus*), like birch, is a white timber (though it has a slight flash in the figure) and can be finished in a similar way.

FINISHES FOR BIRCH

Because the grain grows in both directions, careful preparation is needed. The wood lends itself to natural finishes. Birch has an extremely close texture, so very few coats of finish are required.

BLUE-GREY FINISH

Prepare the surface.

Mix copper sulphate in equal parts, with water.

This produces a blue-grey colour, which looks particularly attractive if wood is selected that has a water-grain pattern (resembling watered silk).

Other stains can be used – but spirit and oil stains tend to produce patchy colours.

ROSEWOOD EFFECT

Stain with mahogany crystals. Leave to dry.

Sand lightly with 320 grit paper.

Apply a coat of white polish.

Mix spirit black with polish and apply with a pencil brush, touching in the rosewood grain pattern to suit. Some practice will be needed to achieve this effect. It is best to copy the pattern from a piece of rosewood veneer.

Use a matt or gloss finish to complete the rosewood effect, either by hand or using a spray gun.

TIPS FOR BIRCH

Apply thin coats.

The grain pattern of birch tends to affect the absorption of stain, resulting in uneven colour.

Before you stain a piece, it is therefore advisable to test the effect on an inconspicuous area or a scrap piece of the same wood.

Beech

Beech

Beech (*Fagus* spp) is grown in Europe, North America and Japan. Variations sometimes occur due to climate and growing conditions. With proper forestry control, it is a sustainable timber. Beech is a hard, very versatile, close-grained wood with an even grain pattern. The colour ranges from a whitish or pale brown to a darker reddish brown. When steamed, beech becomes pink.

The timber is used mainly for furniture – particularly chair frames, as it lends itself to bending or shaping and takes upholstery well. It is also suitable for turning, and is therefore often used` for making turned legs, handles and toys.

For use as a show wood, beech can be stained to imitate other timbers, such as mahogany, walnut and oak, and can then be treated with gloss, matt, pigmented, or water-borne finishes.

FINISHES FOR BEECH

Because beech is a close-grained timber, grain fillers are not necessary. However, cross grain sometimes causes problems, in which case a cabinet scraper can be used during final sanding.

If bleaching is needed to lighten the colour of the wood, you will find that a two-part bleach gives the best results. Two or more applications may be necessary to bleach the timber white.

Natural beech is attractive in its own right, although pigmented stains can be used to obtain an evenly coloured finish or to provide a range of colours, including blue, red and traditional brown. When attempting to match colours using modern finishes, spray tints are useful as they enable you to achieve a very accurate match.

Although beech stains well, solvent wood dyes can bite into it, causing a dark effect in the grain. End grain should be sealed with thinned shellac polish to prevent stain penetrating too deeply and darkening the wood too much.

MAHOGANY FINISH

Prepare the surface.

Stain the timber, using 2 tablespoons of mahogany crystals to 0.5l (1pt) of water, then leave to dry.

Sand lightly, using 320 grit paper.

Apply a coat of polish.

Colour matching will probably be necessary. Mix spirit black and Bismarck brown with polish to make a warm brown colour. Apply with a mop and a pencil brush.

Body up, and leave to dry.

Cut back with 320 grit paper, then stiff off.

This will produce a full-grained, gloss mahogany finish.

ROSEWOOD AND WALNUT FINISHES

The same process can be carried out using other stains and colours. Use spirit colours and pigments to give an even colour.

For rosewood and walnut, stain to the background colour and simulate the grain using a pencil brush and spirit colours.

Practise on a scrap piece of the relevant wood before staining.

Obeche and similar timbers

Obeche (*Triplochiston scleroxylon*) is one of a group of tropical timbers that includes jelutong (*Dyera costulata*), ramin (*Gonystylus macrophyllum*) and rubbertree (*Hevea brasiliensis*). They are all now frequently used for furniture, since they are relatively cheap and, as they grow quite quickly, can be replaced by appropriate forestry methods. They machine well and are easy to work by hand. Because they are sustainable and versatile, this group of timbers is likely to become increasingly popular in the future.

These timbers have a flecked grain pattern rather than a figure. They range in colour from white to a yellowish tint. The colour of the individual species is fairly consistent, so there is little

Obeche   *Jelutong*

difference from one piece to another. Since the grain is bland and featureless, the finisher has the challenge of finding the right techniques to make the timber attractive and interesting. Nevertheless, these woods have good finishing properties and are useful for simulating exotic timbers that are in less plentiful supply.

A certain amount of practice and experimentation is needed in order to learn how to make the most of these timbers – so, unless you have experience of working with them, try out stains and colours on scrap before attempting to finish a workpiece.

FINISHES FOR RUBBERTREE

Formerly, once the latex had been tapped, rubbertrees were cut down and burnt, but now the timber is being used for furniture production. Rubbertree is white with dark-brown flecks, has a close grain, and polishes well. It takes stains but is not very porous, so the best results are obtained with solvent wood dyes. Grain filling is not necessary.

The final finish can either be gloss or matt satin. Modern finishes and matching spray tints can be used to imitate mahogany, oak and walnut. To simulate walnut convincingly, you may need to add figuring, using a mop and a pencil brush.

FINISHES FOR JELUTONG

Jelutong is a soft yellow timber that is good for carving. It can also be used to simulate oak and mahogany. Because of its grain structure, a suitably coloured grain filler should be used. Gloss and matt finishes both give pleasing results.

Pine and similar woods

Most pines (*Pinus* spp) and similar woods such as firs (*Abies* spp) and spruces (*Picea* spp) originate in the northern hemisphere, though some species come from elsewhere – for example, parana pine (*Araucaria*) is native to South America. They grow quickly and, with proper forestry management, can be easily replaced. These timbers are widely employed in building and joinery, and nowadays are being used more and more

Sitka spruce

Yellow pine

in the production of furniture. They can be used in solid or veneer form, or as core timbers faced with hardwood veneers. With appropriate finishing it is possible to enhance and improve the appearance of these woods.

TYPES OF PINES, FIRS AND SPRUCES

The commercial timbers have a variety of names, which do not always reflect their botanical origin. In fact, sometimes timber sold under a particular name may come from more than one species. Names in common use include:

White pine

Timbers sold as "white pine" (*Pinus strobus, Picea abies, Podocarpus dacrydioides*) have a fine grain and can be finished with tinted sealers or polishes to resemble mahogany. They are used for joinery and for painted or pigmented finishes. Always apply thin coats and rub completely flat, with fine (320 grit) abrasive paper to avoid leaving scratch marks as the wood is very soft. Two-part finishes can be used for greater protection.

Sugar pine

(*Pinus lambertiana*) A Californian pine that has practically all the characteristics of "white pine". Used for interior and exterior joinery, piano keys and pattern making. Tends to absorb stains unevenly because of the grain structure, although pigment-suspension stains can

be used to enhance the natural appearance of the wood. Thinly coated satin and matt finishes are recommended. Wax finishes and NC lacquers give good results.

Scots pine

(*Pinus sylvestris*) Also referred to as red deal or European redwood, this light-coloured pine has a distinctive figure with a reddish or yellowish grain pattern. Scots pine is used for interior and exterior joinery, and for inexpensive pine furniture. It can be stained and takes finishes well, including wax and thin matt finishes. Water-borne finishes are good for producing a natural look.

Southern or yellow pine

(*Pinus strobus, Pinus palustris*) The timbers in this group are sold under a bewildering variety of names. The

name used depends on where they are grown. They are generally pale yellow to pale brown, but stains do not penetrate the resinous streaks present in the timber, so colour matching is often needed. Natural-looking wax or thin matt finishes are recommended. An abraded matt finish looks attractive on these woods.

Douglas fir

(*Pseudotsuga menziesii*) Also known as British Columbian or Oregon pine. Has a pronounced grain pattern and a reddish colour. Takes solvent wood dyes well, but not water or chemical stains.

White fir

(*Abies amabilis, Abies grandis, Picea abies*) Has a subdued grain pattern, but with careful selection can be used with brown or mahogany finishes.

Sitka spruce

(*Picea sitchensis*) The wood has a natural springiness. Can be stained, but is better finished naturally as staining tends to look patchy.

Norway spruce

(*Picea abies, Abies alba*) Also known as white deal or European whitewood, this timber is used mainly for interior purposes, as it is not sufficiently durable for outdoor use. It has a distinct grain pattern, with areas of light brown contrasting with the basic white colour. The wood tends to look patchy when stained, due to uneven absorption. However, this can be overcome by using tinted sealers or polishes. Looks best with a thin satin or matt finish. Two-part finishes sometimes produce red blotches.

FINISHES FOR PINE

The colour of pine can range from white or yellow to shades of pink, and depends more on the species than on the climate. Light-coloured varieties are ideal for painted finishes, since not many coats are needed to produce a white or pastel finish. Some species have a pronounced grain pattern, which is produced by the growth rings.

Preparation is important, as the grain structure varies considerably. Use fine grades of paper during final sanding. When cutting back coats of finish, always sand right back until it looks as if the finish has been removed. The smoother the surface, the better the finish. Before using two-part finishes, apply a barrier coat of shellac sealer or a rubber of polish colour.

Timbers like pine can be stained with solvent wood dyes or water stains; spirit stains tend to look patchy. Pigment-suspension stains may be used to simulate other woods, and can produce some interesting effects. Matt or satin finishes are recommended (high-gloss finishes tend not to look so good).

If the wood has a bold grain, colour matching may be necessary. Select a natural-brown spirit stain, to bring out the character of the timber, and apply it with a soft cloth.

Water-based finishes are often extremely effective on pines, producing a natural "unfinished" look to the wood.

Bright colours such as red and blue can also be used, although it is wise to experiment first. In fact, it is always best before any kind of colouring to try out stains or dyes on a small scrap of the same timber.

NATURAL FINISH FOR PINE TABLES

Prepare the surface.

Apply stain as required. Leave to dry.

Apply a clear sanding sealer. Leave to dry.

Cut back with 320 grit paper.

This produces a tough natural finish.

SCRUBBED PINE

Prepare the surface.

Apply a coat of button polish or a light-brown solvent wood dye. Leave to dry.

Thin a cream-coloured paint to 20 per cent and apply it to the surface. Leave to dry.

Sand lightly, using 320 grit paper.

Apply a matt varnish or a wax polish, as required.

This will produce a washed effect, similar to a faded pine finish.

ANTIQUE PINE

Prepare the surface.

Apply a dark solvent wood dye. Leave to dry.

Rub areas such as edges where wear usually occurs with 00 wire wool (see pages 20-21).

Dust off and apply a coat of sanding sealer. Leave to dry.

Denib, using 320 grit paper.

Apply a coat of matt nitrocellulose finish.

TIPS FOR PINE

Always check softwood veneers for glue percolation, which can cause problems, and make sure any glue marks are removed before finishing. Since glue is often light in colour, like the timber, it tends to be difficult to see. The best way to detect glue marks is to look across the surface to see them against the light.

Because pine and similar timbers tend to be soft, a tough good-quality finish is recommended when they are used for table tops. Matt polyurethane finishes are suitable for this purpose.

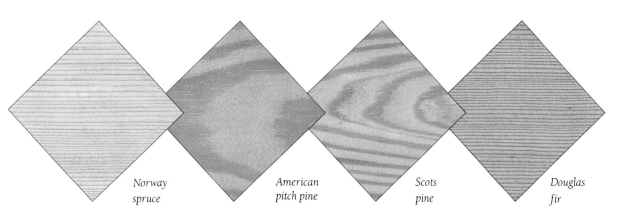

Norway spruce

American pitch pine

Scots pine

Douglas fir

TROUBLESHOOTING

Traditional finishing faults

Although some faults in traditional finishes are due to workshop conditions or the material itself, the majority are caused by human error. Practice is therefore the most effective preventive measure. Fortunately, most traditional finishes (with the exception of varnishes) are reversible and can be rubbed off, without having to resort to stripping and starting again. Oiling and waxing are relatively straightforward finishes, compared with French polishing. The lack of faults catalogued here for those methods reflects their ease of application.

White in the grain

SYMPTOM: White flecks in the grain, under the finish.

CAUSE: Grain filler has not dried, or is too light.

CURE: Rub off polish with methylated spirits; clean off oil and wax with white spirit. Then work out the filler with a stiff brush.

PREVENTION: Make sure filler is dry, or use darker filler.

Ropy surface

SYMPTOM: Waves are visible on the surface after polishing, often in tight circles like ripples. Can also look like rope.

CAUSE: Misuse of polishing rubber.

CURE: Cut back with methylated spirits in the polishing rubber.

PREVENTION: Make sure an even pressure is maintained when using the rubber. Work with circular motions, trying to keep the pressure the same as you move the polishing rubber away from and towards the body.

Cracking

SYMPTOM: Thin cracks show up in the surface after some time has elapsed.

CAUSE: Linseed oil buried under the finish.

CURE: Gently sand the surface with fine abrasive and repolish. If there is extensive cracking, cut back with methylated spirits and rework.

PREVENTION: As for sweating, use less linseed oil on the polishing rubber and avoid burying oil under heavy coats of polish.

Cracking

Sweating

SYMPTOM: Polish remains sticky, even after some time has elapsed.

CAUSE: Linseed oil has been trapped under the finish. Or old white, transparent or pale French polish has been used.

CURE: Cut back the finish with methylated spirits in the polishing rubber, then leave the surface to dry and rework the finish.

PREVENTION: Use less linseed oil to lubricate the polishing rubber, and avoid burying oil under heavy coats of polish.

Blushing

SYMPTOM: A dull whiteness, which can appear in any type of finish.

CAUSE: Damp, cold workshop conditions.

CURE: Cut back and rework.

PREVENTION: Check workshop for damp, and make sure the temperature is not below 18°C (65°F).

Blooming

SYMPTOM: A film of condensation appears in the finished surface.

CAUSE: Humidity in the workshop.

CURE: Sand back and rework.

PREVENTION: Check the level of humidity in your workshop and make sure there is adequate ventilation. If necessary, buy a dehumidifier.

Blooming

Crazing

SYMPTOM: Very fine cracks on the surface.

CAUSE: Too much oil has been used to lubricate the polishing rubber.

CURE: Sand back with fine abrasive paper, and repolish. If the crazing is severe strip off the polish, and repolish.

PREVENTION: Before tackling the surface with the rubber, ensure excess oil is worked out by pressing down with the rubber on a scrap of paper or spare piece of timber.

Crazing

Fatty edges

SYMPTOM: Polish builds up along the edges of table tops and the corners of legs.

CAUSE: As the polishing rubber is squeezed over the edges, polish builds up there.

CURE: Rub down with fine abrasive paper, then touch up and repolish.

PREVENTION: Use the polishing rubber to remove excess polish before it builds up.

Whips

SYMPTOM: Polish builds up in ridges, often in circles following the path of the polishing rubber.

CAUSE: The polishing rubber is too wet.

CURE: Leave to dry. Then sand with fine abrasive, or use a rubber with a little methylated spirits and work until the surface has been levelled.

PREVENTION: Avoid charging the rubber with too much polish.

White edges

SYMPTOM: Edges look as if they are white, where the stain has been worn away.

CAUSE: The surface has been sanded clumsily after applying a water stain.

CURE: Apply polish as normal, then touch up with spirit colours or pigments once the surface is completely dry.

PREVENTION: Take care when sanding stained surfaces, avoiding pressing too hard.

Flaking

SYMPTOM: Film of finish breaks down with time.

CAUSE: Too much oil in a stain or filler.

CURE: Strip and respray.

PREVENTION: Check that lacquer is compatible with filler, stain or stopper.

Chilling

SYMPTOM: Appears as a dull, white semi-opaque film.

Chilling

CAUSE: Cold workshop conditions.

CURE: Repolish the surface using a little methylated spirits in the polishing rubber.

PREVENTION: Ensure the temperature in the workshop does not drop below 18°C (65°F).

HINTS AND TIPS

- Always leave the finish to dry before attempting to deal with faults.

- Apply thin coats of finish, rather than fewer thick coats.

- Always use materials as specified by the suppliers.

- Before taking remedial action, think out what may have gone wrong and check possible causes.

- When spraying only use those thinners recommended by the supplier.

- When spraying with two-part finishes, make sure the right catalyst is used in the correct proportions.

Spray finishing faults

It is often said that one of the skills of the finisher is the knack of remedying a fault without its showing. The ideal is, of course, not to make any mistakes – and prevention is always better than cure!

The more traditional finishes are often reversible, which means they can be removed fairly easily, without recourse to stripping or sanding back. Spray finishes are tougher, and are usually non-reversible. As a result, stripping may be the only cure for a major mistake. You therefore need to be aware of the preventive measures that can be taken to reduce the likelihood of faults.

Air leaks

SYMPTOM: Air hisses out of air holes in air cap.

POSSIBLE CAUSES: Foreign matter in valve; worn or damaged air valve; broken air-valve spring; valve stem needs lubrication; bent valve stem; packing nut too tight; casket damaged or omitted.

CURE: Check and repair parts.

PREVENTION: Maintain and clean spray gun regularly.

Spray fog

SYMPTOM: Spray comes out of the gun as a mist.

POSSIBLE CAUSES: Material too thin; air pressure too high; gun held too far from surface.

PREVENTION: Add more base coat – or start again, using less thinner; reduce air pressure at regulator; hold gun closer to surface.

Pinholes

SYMPTOM: Tiny indentations or pinpricks are formed in the surface of the lacquer as it dries.

Pinholes

CAUSE: The lacquer is applied too heavily, which means that solvents are trapped underneath the surface and have to rise to the top to evaporate.

CURE: Sand back the surface and start again.

PREVENTION: Mix a thinner coat of lacquer; move the spray gun faster across the surface and increase the distance between gun and workpiece.

Overspray

SYMPTOM: The surface feels rough because the spray lies on the surface, forming small particles of dry paint or lacquer.

CAUSE: Insufficient care when using the spraygun.

CURE: Lightly sand the surface with fine abrasive paper, and respray.

PREVENTION: Trigger off after each stroke or pass. Use low air pressure.

Overspray

Fluttering spray

SYMPTOM: Air and material flow is hesitant or jerky.

POSSIBLE CAUSES: Insufficient material in container; canister tipped too far; fluid passage blocked; cracked fluid tube in canister; damaged tip or nozzle; material too heavy; clogged air vent in cup lid; damaged hose or dirty coupling nut; fault in trigger adjustment.

CURE: Check and mend part, or thin the material.

PREVENTION: Keep spray gun well maintained, and clean it thoroughly after use. Mix lacquer according to the manufacturer's instructions.

Fluid leaks

SYMPTOM: The finish leaks out through the nozzle of the gun.

POSSIBLE CAUSES: Dirty or worn fluid tip and nozzle; obstruction causing improper seating of needle; needle packing-nut too tight; broken fluid-needle spring; wrong needle.

CURE: Check, and adjust or replace part.

PREVENTION: Clean spray gun thoroughly, and lubricate moving parts.

Orange-peel effect

SYMPTOM: A slight ripple effect is left on the surface, like orange or lemon peel.

POSSIBLE CAUSES: Spraying too close to the surface; application too thick.

CURE: Rub the surface flat with progressive grades of abrasive, then recoat.

PREVENTION: Keep correct distance between gun and surface, about 200mm (8in), all the time; thin the lacquer, but without using too much thinner.

Orange-peel effect

Cissing

SYMPTOM: Small circular patches, resembling miniature volcanos.

CAUSE: Grease or silicone in the finish repels subsequent coats.

CURE: Deep sand and respray.

PREVENTION: Prepare surface thoroughly before beginning to spray.

Cissing

Blushing

SYMPTOM: A dull whiteness appears in the coat.

CAUSE: Damp workshop conditions.

CURE: strip surface and start again.

PREVENTION: Keep minimum temperature above 18°C (65°F); insulate workshop to reduce humidity.

Runs

SYMPTOM: The finish runs down the surface.

POSSIBLE CAUSES: Holding the gun too close; applying too much material in one place; spraying over the same area twice.

CURE: Leave to dry, and then sand down with fine silicon-carbide paper before respraying.

PREVENTION: Hold gun further from surface; practise a consistent sweep over the piece, overlapping by no more than 50 per cent on each sweep.

Aeration

SYMPTOM: Small bubbles appear, creating a milky effect.

POSSIBLE CAUSES: Too heavy a coat of lacquer (which traps air or solvent under the surface); or too much air pressure, which can dry the surface too quickly for solvent to evaporate or air to escape.

CURE: Spray on a wet-flow coat; or pullover the surface and then respray.

PREVENTION: Keep spray gun moving, and make sure it is not too close to the surface.

Blistering

SYMPTOM: Small blisters on the surface.

CAUSE: Water or grease in the air line getting into the atomized material.

CURE: Sand surface and respray.

PREVENTION: Clean air line and drain transformer.

Blistering

Blooming

SYMPTOM: Film of condensation on the surface.

CAUSE: Humidity in the workshop.

CURE: strip surface and start again.

PREVENTION: Use a dehumidifier in the workshop, and keep the area well ventilated.

Wrinkling or cracking

SYMPTOM: Unwanted cracks or wrinkles appear in the finish.

CAUSE: When a second coat of lacquer is applied before the first has dried properly, the two finishes dry at different rates.

CURE: Sand and respray; or strip and start again if the cracks are deep.

PREVENTION: Check the finish manufacturer's instructions for drying, thinning and curing. Make sure the first coat is dry before applying the second.

Flaking

SYMPTOM: Finish breaks up.

CAUSE: Too much oil in filler or stain.

CURE: Strip back, then brush out filler and start again.

PREVENTION: Make sure the filler or stain is compatible with the finish.

White in the grain

SYMPTOM: White flecks under the finish.

CAUSE: Filler has not dried thoroughly. Or the fault has been caused by incompatibility between the filler and the finish.

CURE: Strip and respray.

PREVENTION: Make sure excess filler is cleaned off, and that it is completely dry before spraying.

White in the grain

H E A L T H   A N D   S A F E T Y

Some of the materials used for finishing are dangerous – indeed, many of them are poisonous, flammable or corrosive – so always take care when using or handling them. Store materials safely, and make sure that waste is disposed of in the proper manner. Fire precautions must be taken at all times, and protective clothing worn in case of spillage.

One important safety rule is that finishes must never be stored in or decanted into a food container or anything that resembles one. Milk bottles, saucers and ice-cream cartons mean food to adults as well as children – and it may be too late when someone realizes that the contents are not what he or she expected.

Protective clothing and equipment

Hands are the most frequent victims of chemicals. When using caustic strippers always wear heavy-duty elbow-length industrial gloves, otherwise ordinary PVC gloves are satisfactory. Household rubber gloves can be used for French polishing.

Whenever working with chemicals or in a dusty environment, wear safety goggles to protect your eyes from splashes or irritation. Alternatively, you can use a visor-type face guard, which you may find more comfortable than goggles.

To prevent inhalation of fumes and dust, there are simple masks or more complex battery-powered respirators, some of which have the advantage of incorporating eye protection and filtration (the latter is important when carrying out heavy sanding).

1

2

3

Unless you are embarking on a huge job a simple mask will suit most purposes.

Besides protecting your skin and clothes, overalls reduce the risk of dust, hairs and fibres being transferred from clothing onto the surface of the work during finishing. When spraying, an overall that has a hood is an advantage as it protects your hair from spray. A PVC apron must be worn when working with bleaches, strippers and other chemicals – a cloth apron can be burnt by chemicals and, if that happens, the material may keep burning substances in close contact with your skin.

Noise can be injurious, too. Sanders and other power tools make a deafening whine. Hearing protection is therefore essential when working with them. The best kind of earmuffs are the ones that look like earphones, but it is not always easy to wear them with goggles and a respirator – in which case, earplugs are a serviceable, if less effective, substitute. To prevent loss and ear infections, clean earplugs regularly and keep them in a sealed box when you are not using them.

1 This type of mask has a filter made of gauze which can be thrown away after use.
2 Supplied in packs and useful when sanding, this mask has a nose clip which fastens over the nose to prevent dust being inhaled.
3 A full-face respirator with changeable filter. Use while spraying or sanding to prevent dust and fumes being inhaled.

168

Storing caustic materials

Caustic materials must be stored in a locked cabinet when not being used. Always keep the materials in the container they were supplied in, and make sure the label does not become detached. If it is necessary to decant caustic material, pour it carefully into a non-corrosive container made of glass, plastic or earthenware. If any of the decanted material is left over, do not return it to its original container. Always wear gloves when handling caustic substances.

Labelling containers clearly is an essential safety precaution, but remember that children too young to read may be mobile and inquisitive and hungry or thirsty – so never use food containers, even if clearly labelled.

Waste disposal

Waste materials can and often do retain caustic characteristics. Correct disposal is therefore vital. Do not pour or throw chemicals or finishing materials down the drain – instead, find out from the appropriate authority where and how it is permissible to dispose of them.

Labelling

Do not remove manufacturers' labels from containers. They provide important information and warnings. It is worth dating finishes and other materials for future reference, as some have a finite shelf life and it is safest not to use materials that are past the specified date.

Dust and fumes

Most people realize that fumes are dangerous, but dust should not be underestimated as a health hazard – especially if you or your family suffer from hay fever, asthma or other respiratory diseases. Also, it has been established that wood dust can cause nasal cancer, though the incidence of the disease is primarily among people exposed to large quantities of wood dust. Many of the finishes and strippers that include hydrocarbon solvents can cause dizziness – which may lead to workshop accidents. It therefore makes sense to get into the habit of wearing a mask or respirator, when spraying and sanding.

Before buying a filter for a mask or a respirator, look at the recommended uses on the packet to make sure it will provide effective protection against fine dust and harmful fumes. Some filters are designed to catch coarse dust particles only, and are not adequate for constant use.

Fire precautions

Flammable materials must be stored in a fireproof metal cabinet or a fireproof bin with a lid on it. Storage bins and cabinets need to be kept locked and must display a notice warning that the contents are flammable.

Large quantities of chemicals and other combustible materials have to be stored in a brick building that has a retaining wall. A notice warning of the fire hazard must be prominently displayed on the exterior of the building. If you need more detailed information about regulations concerning flammable materials or about fire protection, contact the fire service, who will be glad to advise.

For effective fire prevention, position fire blankets, extinguishers, and fire buckets filled with sand (for dealing with spillages) around the workshop. A good-quality fire extinguisher that can cope with the relevant categories of fire is essential. Display a NO SMOKING sign and fit a smoke detector (or more than one in a large workshop).

Keep the workshop as clean as possible. Dust constitutes a fire hazard. In the event of an explosion in the workshop, fine dust is likely to be whipped out of nooks and crannies and blown around in clouds that can easily ignite. Secondary explosions caused by dust clouds can inflict greater damage and worse burns than the initial blast.

Common sense is good protection. Naked flames must never be permitted in the vicinity of flammable substances; and food or drink must never be consumed when there are poisonous materials around. But even seemingly harmless substances can be potentially dangerous. Linseed oil, for example, dries by oxidation, which can cause a piece of cloth to heat and spontaneously ignite. Never throw rolled-up cloths soaked in linseed into a waste bin – instead, put them in a bucket of water, then dispose of them safely. If they are not being used for the moment but may be needed for further work, unroll them and allow them to dry outdoors. Two-part finishes also present a fire hazard, since they heat up during the curing process, and should always be used with care.

GLOSSARY

Acetic acid (white vinegar) Used to *neutralize* two-pack bleaches.

Acid-catalyst lacquers A lacquer usually based on urea formaldehyde and melamine which cures chemically after the addition of a hardener. Can be applied with a brush, spray or roller. Available in clear, gloss, matt and may be coloured.

Bars Metric measure of pressure.

Bevelling Taking off sharp edges with a plane or with a chisel.

Binder This is the solid content of a varnish or lacquer remaining after the solvent has evaporated and which forms the film, and if pigments are added binds them to the surface.

Bodying up The stage in *French polishing* when the polish is built up to give depth to the finish.

Buffing Using a soft mop or cloth to produce a gloss finish.

Burnisher A tool used to produce a *burr* on a cabinet scraper by drawing the burnisher along the edge of the scraper at an angle of 5°.

Burnishing cream A fine abrasive cream applied with pressure using a soft cloth to produce a high gloss finish.

Burr The fine hook of steel along the edge of a cabinet scraper, used for scraping fine shavings from the surface.

Button polish Golden brown polish made from methylated spirits and *shellac*; made in the shape of buttons.

Carnauba wax Hard wax with a high melting point used for floor polishes. A mixture of beeswax and carnauba wax is used in turning.

Cellulose lacquers Fast drying nitrocellulose finishes often used for spraying. Supplied in gloss or matt and clear or coloured.

Cellulose thinners Solvents used to thin *cellulose lacquers* and clean equipment. Use thinners and lacquers made by the same manufacturer.

Chemical stains Chemicals that are dissolved in water and, when applied to the surface, change the colour of the timber by chemical reaction.

Chemical stripping The procedure of removing old finishes using solvent, paint and varnish removers or strong alkaline solutions. Hot-air guns may also be used but may scorch the wood.

Cleat A small nail or screw used to hold down a panel on the bench while the panel is being worked on.

Cobweb A spraying fault that occurs when sprayed *shellac* materials do not atomize properly and form a cobweb pattern on the surface.

Cold cure See *Acid-catalyst lacquers*.

Colour mop Round-shaped brush made from soft bristles, supplied in sizes 6–10, used for applying colour.

Cramping Using a cramp for pressure when gluing joints and repairing blisters.

Creep The way stain is absorbed along the grain.

Cross grain Grain structure that runs at an angle to the main grain direction. Sanding across the grain is usually to be avoided.

Cut back Rubbing a finish with fine abrasive paper until the finish is flat and smooth.

Danish oil An oil finish that cures by oxidation (reaction with oxygen). Particularly useful for oily timbers.

Denibbing Removing by rubbing with a fine abrasive paper to remove any small particles of foreign matter which stand proud on a dry surface coating.

Distressing Making a piece of furniture look old by bruising the surface and giving it a faded appearance.

Doping Application of dope, which is a mixture of *dye*, *pigment* and *French polish*, using a *mop* or brush to make a semi-transparent colour.

Dye A liquid that will alter the colour of wood without leaving a surface film or obscuring the grain. Spirit soluble dyes are made by dissolving analine dyes in methylated spirits. Solvent wood dyes are made from oil soluble dye stuffs, usually white spirit or naphtha. Water soluble dyes are made from dye stuffs soluble in water.

Fad A pear-shaped piece of wadding used to apply *French polish* to nooks and crannies and also as the core of a *polishing rubber*.

Fadding Applying *French polish* with a *fad* before *bodying up*.

Fillers and grain fillers A mixture of filling powder, binder, solvent and *pigments* applied with hessian to fill the pores in timber.

French polish *Shellac* and methylated spirits mixed to produce a polish, which is also supplied as garnet, white, pale, button and transparent polish.

French polishing General term referring to the application of *shellac* polish with a *polishing rubber*.

Glazes A transparent or translucent coating material, sometimes coloured, applied over a base colour and used for special effects like graining and marbling.

Green copperas A *chemical stain* used to produce green to grey hues.

Grit grades Sizes of grit used on abrasive papers. High numbers, such as 360, refer to fine grit while 80 is a coarse abrasive.

Heartwood The centre of a log that has stopped growing, and is usually darker and harder than the outer layer of *sapwood*.

Keying Abrading the surface of a finish to roughen it as a base for further coats of finish.

Medium density fibreboard (MDF) Fibreboard, similar to chipboard, but denser. Made from wood dust bonded by a resin.

Medullary rays Grain pattern in oak that runs across the grain, contrasting with the rest of the timber. The pattern is enhanced by quarter-sawing the timber.

Neutralize To make chemically neutral (neither acidic nor alkaline).

Nigrosine water stain Traditional *water stain*, giving a black colour for ebonizing.

Oiling Process of applying oil to produce an oiled finish; for example, Danish or linseed oil applied to teak.

Oxalic acid crystals White crystals used as a mild bleach, when in *saturated solution*, to clean off iron or blue stains.

Pigments Colours that do not dissolve, but are suspended in a medium to produce opaque colours. Mixed with paints, scumbles and *glazes*.

Pigment suspension stain Semi-transparent stain made from finely ground colours that remain in suspension.

Polishing rubber A *fad* wrapped in a white cotton cloth, used for *French polishing*.

Polyester resin Two-part resin finish, which cures by chemical reaction, with one part acting as a catalyst.

Polymerization This is the chemical reaction which occurs whereby the molecules link, often by cross-linking with various components, to form a polymer. See *Acid Catalyst Lacquers*.

Polyurethane oil Synthetic oil finish.

Proprietary reviver Used for rejuvenating old finishes; sold as polish or finish reviver.

Pumice powder Fine abrasive powder for dulling. Used with a dulling brush.

Raising the grain Wetting timber to expand the cells of the wood before applying a finish.

Sanding sealer A sealer that incorporates a sanding agent to make sanding easier.

Sapwood Layer of timber surrounding the *heartwood* which carries the sap through the tree.

Saturated solution When no more solid material can be dissolved in a solution.

Scumbles A semi-transparent stain for application over an opaque base of paint.

Sealing coat First coat of finish used to seal the surface of the timber before applying further coats.

Shellac A resin secreted by the lac beetle which is only soluble in alcohol or an alkaline solution of water. When dissolved in alcohol it is known as *French polish*.

Shellac sanding sealer Sealer with *shellac* base which includes a sanding agent to fill the pores of the grain.

Skein wadding Fine wadding covered in thin paper and used as the core of the *polishing rubber*.

Solvent wood dyes; spirit colours; spirit aniline dyes Dyes that are dissolved in either alcohol or methylated spirits to produce translucent colours.

Spiriting off Stage of *French polishing* when the *polishing rubber* is charged with methylated spirits to produce a gloss finish.

Stain See *dye*, but exterior wood stains are film formers containing pigments and are not for use under other finishes.

Stiffing off Stage of *French polishing* when straight strokes are used, following the grain, with the *polishing rubber* charged with diluted polish and methylated spirits.

Stoppers Materials used to fill holes and deep bruises. Available as wax stopper, shellac stopper and two-pack stopper.

Thinner Solvent used to thin finishes.

Thixotropic agent Additive to paints and varnishes to increase viscosity and prevent pigments settling and to reduce the chance of runs.

Transparent polish Made from *shellac* that has been bleached and de-waxed to produce a very pale amber *shellac* solution.

Tung oil Vegetable oil for oil finishes, also used in some paints and lacquers.

Urea formaldehyde glue Resin glue used in modern furniture and often supplied in powder form which is then mixed with water.

Varnish stains Varnish mixed with a *dye* or *pigments* and supplied in a range of colours.

Varnish A transparent coating based on a mixture of resins and drying oils and a solvent.

Water stain *Stain* made from water soluble *dyes*.

Wax stains Wax and *stain* combination available in a range of colours, producing a coloured wax effect.

Wax sticks Coloured wax *stopper* made from wax and *pigments*, for filling small dents and bruises.

Wet and dry abrasive Abrasive paper made from silicon carbide that uses water as a lubricant. Self-lubricating abrasives incorporate a powder to take away the dust which can scratch the surface.

White polish *French polish* using bleached *shellac* for natural or light-coloured finishes.

White spirit Hydrocarbon solvent used to thin oil stains, scumbles, gold size and *glazes*.

INDEX

Page numbers in *italics* indicate illustrations

USEFUL NAMES AND ADDRESSES

Suppliers of equipment (veneers, tools, polishes etc) to furniture trade. Mail order available.
FINE ART VENEERS CO LTD
Industrial Estate
Mildenhall
Suffolk IP28 7AY
0638 712550

Waxes, shellac products, stains, acid-catalyst lacquers etc. Mail order available.
FIDDES & SON
Florence Works
Brindley Road
Cardiff
CF1 7TX
0222 340323

General suppliers of wood finishing products. Mail order available.
JOHN MYLAND LTD
80 Norwood High Street
London SE27 9NW
081 670 9161

General suppliers of wood finishing products. Mail order available.
W S JENKINS LTD
Jeco Works
Tariff Road
London N17 OEN
081 808 2336

Wide range of wood finishes and antique restoration products. Mail order available.
LIBERON WAXES
Mountfield Industrial Estate
Leroyd Road
New Romney
Kent TN28 8XU
0679 67555

Manufacturers of wood dyes, fillers, strippers and wood finishes. Mail order available.
RUSTINS LTD
Drayton Works
Waterloo Road
London NW2 7TX
081 450 4666

Produce acrylic aqueous surface coatings. Mail order available.
WESTCOUNTRY FINISHES LTD
The Paint Factory
Pottery Road
Bovey Tracey
Devon TQ13 9DS
0626 833209

Manufacturers and suppliers of brushes.
F A HEFFER & CO LTD
24 The Pavement
London SW4 OJA
071 622 6871

Suppliers of quality tools, machinery and workshop consumables. Mail order available.
AXMINSTER POWER TOOLS
Chard Street
Axminster
Devon EX13 5DZ
0297 33656

General wood finishing supplies (including decorative finishes). Mail order available.
PLOTONS (SUNDRIES) LTD
273 Archway Road
London N6 5AA
081 348 0315

Manufacturers of wood finishes/general and specialist paints. Most wood finishing products available by mail order.
J W BOLLOM LTD
PO Box 78
Croydon Road
Beckenham
Kent BR3 4BL
081 658 2299

Suppliers of paints, wallpapers and brushes etc to decorators trade. No mail order service.
ANGLIAN DECORATORS
SUPPLIES LTD
Anglian House
Claydons Lane
Raleigh
Essex SS6 7UP
0268 773891

Decorative effects supplies a speciality. Mail order available for brushes and tools, but not for paints.
J H RATCLIFFE & CO (PAINTS)
LTD
135A Linaker Street
Southport
PR8 5DF
0704 537999

Suppliers to wood finishing trade (minimum 5 litre/1.3 gallons order). No mail order service.
GRANYTE WOOD FINISHES
Delamare Road
Cheshunt
Waltham Cross
Herts EN8 9SP